LOOK AT ME NOW

by

Thomas J. Hubschman

Savvy Press

Published by:

Savvy Press
PO Box 63
Salem, NY 12865
http://www.savvypress.com

Special thanks to Eric Black
(ericblak@aol.com) for his superb cover art

ISBN: 978-0-9669877-6-8
LCCN: 2007931610

Printed in the United States of America

For L.G.H.

Other books by Thomas J. Hubschman:

The Jew's Wife (Short Story Collection)
Billy Boy (Novel)
Space Ark (Science Fiction)
Alpha-II (Science Fiction)
Leffingwell's Planet (Science Fiction)
The Best of Gowanus: New Writing from Africa, Asia and the Caribbean
(Editor)
*The Best of Gowanus II: More New Writing from Africa, Asia and the
Caribbean* (Editor)

Look at Me Now

I

My Great Escape

Monday, December 15

I've been careful not to remove too much on any given morning. A few pieces of jewelry, some favorite snapshots, a dress or two— whatever fills up half a shopping bag. If my husband questions me I'll say I'm just bringing skirts to the dry cleaner's or dropping off some old clothes at the thrift shop. For the past month I haven't left the house without carrying with me some of this loot, camouflaged by paperwork I've brought home from my job, along with a pair of dress shoes to change into when I get to the office, an extra set of pantyhose.

There's no way of his knowing this will be my last trip and that after today the bed I've been occupying in our son's old room will be permanently empty. No way of his knowing that our marriage, such as it's been, will be over. Unless he looks up from his newspaper and sees the fear on my face, my terror of his discovering at the last moment what I'm up to.

"Still here?" he says from the bedroom doorway, making me jump. I've been awake since four a.m. but didn't dare get up until the alarm went off at seven.

"Just on my way," I say, trying so hard to remember where I've stashed my mother's brooch, and her mother's before her, that my head is aching.

"You look nice," he says. But I don't turn his way, don't want to see the look on his face. Not this morning. "You have a nice shape."

"Thanks."

"Misplaced something?"

"My mother's brooch. The silver one with diamond chips. I want to drop it off at the jeweler's, see how much it costs to have it cleaned."

Half truths are the best lies, I've learned. Usually at this time he's buried deep in the *Times* or one of the scholarly journals he still subscribes to. Any other day he just grunts as I leave, maybe adding "Late night?" meaning will he have to fix his own supper while I supposedly attend a union meeting or lecture. I tell myself he can't really know this is it, but something about my body language or the smell of my fear has alerted him, alerted and aroused him.

"Not very late, no," I say, remembering suddenly the brooch is in our safe deposit box. I have a key, but there's another hanging from a nail by the kitchen sink. I'll have to get to the safe deposit box and remove the brooch before he does. He can keep the rest of what's in there. "I'm off."

He doesn't budge. I can't get by without squeezing up against him. This isn't the first time he's blocked my path, making me feel trapped and dependent on him for the privilege of moving freely about my own home. But what he wants this morning is more than acknowledgement of his authority, and he wants it freely given besides.

"No time," I say, my heart hammering so hard I'm afraid he'll hear it. "I have a meeting in"—I make a production out of checking my oversized watch—"forty-five minutes."

"I'm a fast worker."

I stand holding the Macy's bag half full of the few last dear things

I dare take with me. I avoid his big green eyes made twice as large by the thick glasses he's worn since adolescence. I'd see too much in them, too much of myself, of us. I'd see twenty-three years and not all of them bad. Even now we have good moments. I still laugh at his jokes, most of them, and he seems just as good-looking as he ever did despite the weight he's put on. I remind myself I'm not leaving because I don't love him anymore but because I do, because love, what's left of it, is my shackle. If I stay I can only be who *he* wants me to be, and even then only when he wants me to be it.

He takes a step to one side and I dart past as if he's a stranger blocking my way into a subway car. He laughs. With the apartment door now just a few feet away I can laugh too.

April fourth. Two weeks till my seventeenth birthday. Cold, rainy. The cruelest month, we learned just that week in Mr. Shapiro's English class.

"Miss Finley?" he says in the same tone he uses when he calls out the best test scores, 'Miss Finley, ninety-eight. Excellent work.' "Miss Finley," he says this morning, looking up—he can't see much better than my father, so he doesn't usually bother to look up—"please report to Mr. Lewis's office." The "please" and "Mr. Lewis's" instead of "the principal's" is out of deference to all those A's and A-pluses. I don't notice at the time (my heart still pounds whenever anyone calls out my name in public) but afterward, ever after, I recall that he turned quite red, because he knew. They all knew—Shapiro, Miss Flaherty, Mr. Greenblatt, even Ivan the terrible gym teacher who was always threatening to fail me.

Every head in the room turns my way, though I don't notice this either until after it's over. I walk numb out of the classroom. Mr. Shapiro has already resumed talking about free verse just as if his star pupil has merely gone to the john. His baritone follows me down the deserted corridor. 'April is the cruelest month, Miss Finley. Gather ye rosebuds while ye may.'

I expect to find Tim Davis in the principal's office, but the three heavy blond chairs in the waiting area are empty. I want to face this with Tim. After all, we did it together.

"Have a seat," the troll who guards Lewis's door says, extending a fat freckled arm toward the empty chairs without looking up. Her cheap bracelets jiggle obscenely. Alice Falcone says the woman gives Lewis blow jobs during lunch hour. Lewis is gray but not bad-looking, not disgusting like some of the other male teachers. He could do better than Faye Rosenberg.

'April is the cruelest month, breeding lilacs out of the dead land...' I can memorize most poetry at will, even long poems. Eliot's is stupid, I think, the hard chair wide enough for two or three of me, I feel like I'm back in kindergarten. Stupid poetry for fat, stupid, middle-aged men. Give me Herrick any day. 'Gather ye rosebuds, Miss Finley.' And that's what I did. That's why I'm sitting where I am this morning.

"Mr. Lewis will see you now," the troll says, though there's been no communication between herself and the principal since I arrived. She was just busting my chops, impressing on me the gravity of the audience I'm about to be accorded.

"Thank you so much," I say, giving her my aunt Bella's I'm-a-doctor's-wife-and-you're-not smile.

"Have a seat, Miss Finley," Lewis says without looking up from the papers he's signing on his big dark-wood desk. His pate, I note, is almost bald, and I had thought him the one decent-looking man on the entire faculty.

I almost trip on the wall-to-wall but make it safely to the chair in front of his desk. I sit down and smooth my dress over my thighs just as if I weren't already showing, but my hands are trembling. I lock them on my lap, then plant them face down, but he still doesn't look up.

"Just one more second and I'll be with you."

All I can think is, Why isn't Tim here? Why isn't my mother? I feel like I used to in first grade when I had to cross the Grand Concourse on my own, abandoned to a world I couldn't hope to negotiate, much less control. I have to fight back tears of outrage and self-pity just as I did then.

"So," he says finally, glancing at my swollen stomach and only then into my my face. I blink away the blur of tears and see that he's turned quite red. Have I disgraced him, disgraced the school? "You're a good student, Miss Finley. An excellent student," he adds as if despite his better judgment. Then he turns even more red and looks down. "I can't tell you how sorry I am it's...come to this. I'm sure your parents are as well. But of course my hands are tied," he says but promptly runs one of them through his thinning hair.

This sounds like the prelude to a suspension, probably until well after the baby is born sometime in late June. I will no longer be allowed to attend classes. I will have to do all the work at home, get a tutor if need be. I never expected to attend classes nine months pregnant.

"I'm sorry," he says, making an effort to look me in the eye, "very sorry."

I see how difficult this is for him. I sense he would have preferred to handle it some other way. But then he says, "The decision to expel you comes from the chancellor's office. I had no voice in the matter."

I can't take it in at first. It's one thing to put me out of sight, pretend that nice girls don't engage in the kind of activity that results in my present condition. But expulsion is what happens to incorrigibles, chronic truants, students who physically assault faculty. Who have I hurt but myself?

"High school should be a time for applying oneself academically. Having fun as well. But within bounds. If you step outside those bounds you have to be prepared to suffer the consequences."

His eyes are fixed well above my head. It's not until long after the interview is over that I realize what a disgusting worm he is. All I think now is: I'm expelled. No decent college will accept me. I don't realize my troubles will just be starting when the baby is born. I still think of its birth as being the end of my nightmare. The worst I imagined was that I would miss the senior prom, which I had no intention of attending anyway, Tim and I already decided we would go to a movie. And I couldn't care less about graduation.

He goes on about respecting oneself and saving one's virtue for one's wedding night. I feel myself shrinking, becoming less and less of who I was, who I might have been. Only a small voice inside fights back. It says, Why isn't my mother here? Why am I going through this alone?

He finishes his speech. He's just sitting, waiting. For what.

"But," I begin because I must say something, though I have no clue what it should be because I have all but ceased to exist. It's that small voice inside who is talking, talking through me, "I only did it with *one* boy. The other girls do it with everybody."

His color deepens. My God, I think, I've given him a heart attack. He's staring straight at me, his eyes bugged out and watery. Please God, I pray, don't let him die while he's looking at me like that.

"You may go now, Miss Finley."

I carry that moment with me like a running sore. I don't need psychotherapy to understand how much it's formed me, how much rage I carry, how much I've beat up on myself for being so stupid as to get myself into that kind of situation in the first place. But I also think I deserve points for what I've accomplished despite all that. My son is finally on his own and self-supporting, though it took two hospitalizations and what will probably be a lifelong regimen of medication. And his mother not only got her high school diploma (no GED, a Regents with honors) and college degree but a masters as well. And today, God willing, she's standing up on her hind legs and walking out of a relationship that stopped being a real marriage more than fifteen years ago.

The stairwell smells like every pre-War apartment building I've ever been in, starting with my parents'. The odor migrates from building to building like a lonely ghost, an essence of Irish cabbage, Jewish roasts, Italian pasta and now rice-and-beans and collards. It smells more like home than does the interior of 4B where I, where we, have lived for the last two decades. It smells like first day of school, my own and my child's, I no longer distinguish. It smells like the *Times* on Sunday morning, with bagels from the coffee shop at 96th Street. It smells like my mother's perfume, my father's perspiration.

The white marble stairs are slippery, worn down in the middle like a cathedral's, but I don't dare trust myself to the unreliable elevator. The stairwell's flickering light is barely enough to see by. If I twist an ankle it will be my own fault, so I slow down, concentrate on the last long remaining flight to the building's lobby where a ragged sofa and two dusty armchairs keep up a pretense of respectability.

I reach it just as the elevator clunks to a halt. I freeze like a squirrel caught in somebody's headlights, waiting to see if it's my husband in-side, having finally wised up. But no, it's only Emma from 3C, bright and redhaired and young, young, young.

"Good morning!" she calls as if we meet this way every morning. Her tennis shoes are so white, at first I don't see anything else--the gray ("Smoke") of her pantyhose, her short skirt and floppy turtle-neck. If I'm real, she's not. I see women like her on TV, winning dif-ficult court cases, saving the lives of freckle-faced children. "Getting your exercise this morning?" she says as I calculate the odds whether she's slept with my husband—whether or how often.

"Just didn't want to get trapped in that thing," I say, glancing at the rusty dark hunk of metal she's just emerged from like Snow White from her coffin.

"I only take it myself because I'm lazy."

Her accent is Midwest or upstate, not one she has to worry about. My husband says I have three different accents: a proper one for business and other formal occasions; what he calls my Grand Concourse accent; and my everyday Rocky Graziano dese-and-dose. Not for nothing he almost got a doctorate in linguistics.

But this little butt-twitcher was born with a silver tongue to match her perfect teeth and gorgeous hair. She's only slumming where I've had to raise my crazy kid just a sniper shot from Harlem. She can return to Akron or Topeka anytime she wants and tell amusing tales about her years among quaint aborigines like myself.

"Chilly," she says when we reach the littered sidewalk outside, but she doesn't close her oversize Yankees jacket over her big boobs. She looks up at the patch of blue sky above the gray buildings as if she's just stepped out into a plowed field. Even in the morning light her skin is flawless, not even an old acne scar.

"Goddamn freezing," I reply, pulling the collar of my P-jacket tight around my throat.

"Bus?" she says.

"Subway."

"Well, then," she says, big white smile, no lipstick, none required, "have a nice day," and marches off, her little butt hitching right and left as if 123rd Street were a Parisian runway.

I stand on the broad cracked sidewalk where Kevin tried to learn to ride a two-wheeler until he fell off and broke an arm, the bike promptly put back into the building's basement where it was stolen two months later. I stand where the ambulance waited, its big light revolving the same bright red as the one on the train set my parents gave him for his sixth birthday. I see the look on his face as the paramedics lifted him inside, resigned, forgiving. And ten years later his blank, empty gaze when the ambulance was from Bellevue Psychiatric after he had spent two months rocking back and forth like a Yeshiva boy, finally oblivious to his father's impossible will, not to mention my own attempts, too late, to comfort him.

I tell my legs to get moving, and they do. But a big chunk of me remains. Getting out in one piece may be the easy part. What if I'm like those convicts who can't cope with the big world beyond the walls? What if I come back and bang on my prison door, begging to be let in?

The idea's so scary I quicken my step, miss the curb and almost end up flat on my ass.

"You okay?" asks a nice-looking fellow with a gray mustache.

I tell him, yes, sure. I'm fine, I say, this time only to myself. Tiptop. All systems go.

And pray I mean it.

II

Look at Me Now

The Same Day

"If my husband calls I'm not here," I tell Connie, the switch-board operator. Connie's had to get an order of protection against her own ex, so I don't have to paint a picture for her.

I climb the filthy staircase to my tiny second-floor office that overlooks a Chinese fishmonger's on East Broadway. The smell of fish—fresh, rotten, in-between—never leaves the building. A daily cooking class for clients adds rancid peanut oil to the mix.

I stuff my shopping bag into a drawer of the filing cabinet. The other drawers are already filled with books and underwear. The files that used to be housed there are stacked not-so-neatly on the floor behind my desk.

I barely manage to close the file drawer, but this is the last of the loot. This is my D-Day. Do or die, no going back, all the old clichés, they seem newly minted just for me. I sit down in the busted swivel chair behind the gray metal desk that blocks my doorway to any but the skinniest junkies. I can breathe now. I've made it. Step one.

Step two will be telling Kevin. He's a big boy now, married, with a job that doesn't stress him out too much. He knows what his father is like, suffered the man's abuse himself until he had to be hospitalized. Even so, he's a certified schizophrenic and reacts to change with the same terror that his mother does. I used to think of us as two prisoners sharing the same cell block. I couldn't bust out and leave him behind. I had to wait till he was settled and looked after, and now's my own chance, maybe my last.

My hands are trembling like those Slinkies Kevin used to play with. I can't find the pack of cigarettes in my big Coach bag, then I spill them on the dirty floor. Then my eighty-nine-cent lighter won't work. When the phone rings it's like someone threw a firecracker.

"You got away all right?"

"Barely," I say, pawing through the debris in my bag. Finally I locate a book of matches and manage to get one lit while cradling the phone between my neck and shoulder. I draw the smoke right down to my navel. I don't ever want to exhale.

"You there?"

"Sorry. Just lighting up."

"What comes next?" he says. "Still planning to move into that hotel on the East Side?"

"Till I can find an apartment."

"That won't be easy."

"Tell me about it."

So, why don't you invite me to move in with you? We see each other almost every night. But then I remember if there's one thing I don't want it's to ruin what this man and I have by rushing things. Only, if he asked me I'd say yes in a flash. I haven't wanted someone this bad for twenty years, not since Tim Davis and I started doing it in his mother's apartment after school.

"Come by for dinner?" he says.

"Sure," I say. Dinner and two or three hours of fucking. I've already got my hand between my legs. "See you then."

As I put my Marlboros back in my bag I spot the letter I wrote to my husband and then forgot to leave in the mailbox on my way out of the building this morning. So he's still none the wiser, will expect me home tonight as usual. Right now he's having his morning walk in Riverside Park, checking out the river traffic and the skirts. He still has a taste for coeds, Columbia provides him with a fresh crop every autumn. I don't know how often he scores, probably not anything like when he was still teaching. His students used to throw themselves at him, and I was stupid enough to let him tell me about it, me with a toddler to look after while I was studying for the high school diploma denied me when I got pregnant. I was even flattered to be married to a man that desirable. Which shows how screwed up I must be.

When I don't return home tonight he may just decide to come down to my job. I can call in sick for a couple days, but that would just mean postponing the inevitable. I see now that I haven't really thought this through. All I cared about was getting myself and a few possessions safely out of that apartment. I always assumed there'd be hell to pay even if I managed to do it without his realizing. But what if he turns up at reception and Connie can't keep him from barging up the stairs to confront me? What if our security guard decides it's a domestic matter and chooses not to get involved?

I lock my office door and tell Connie I'm going out for coffee. "I'll be back in ten minutes."

I head for the post office on Canal Street and ask there how long a letter will take to reach West 123rd Street if I mail it Special Delivery.

"Hard to say," is the answer I get from the fat lifer behind the bullet-proof glass.

"Give it your best shot."

"All we guarantee is it will arrive before the regular delivery."

"It's possible it could be delivered tomorrow."

"It's possible."

I rush back toward the treatment center, then remember what I was supposed to be going out for and stop at a sandwich shop to pick up two coffees. While I'm waiting I spot my husband eating a muffin at the far end of the counter. It can't actually be him, he still knows nothing. Unless he's checked my closet or gone through my dresser drawers and seen that all my good jewelry is missing, along with most of my underwear. Besides, I can't see worth a damn beyond six or seven feet. Even so, I make a beeline out of there.

"No calls?" I ask as I hand Connie the extra coffee.

"Thanks," she says. "No, nothing."

I race back upstairs, flop down behind my desk and light another cigarette. All right, I tell myself, let's consider our options. But all that comes to mind is the image of my husband, all six foot two inches of him, making like King Kong. How could I do this to him, he says even before he actually speaks. You little slut, he says, though it was he who started fooling around long before I did, and even then I was only doing it with one man at a time. I only took a lover because I couldn't bear the humiliation of his own infidelities. The man I'm seeing now is just my second if you discount the one-night stands, and there weren't that many of them.

Knock, knock. But it's only Laura, the other Employment Specialist. "Hey, kid," she says, sitting down in the client's chair and reaching for one of my Marlboros. Laura is ten years older than me, divorced, lives alone in a studio apartment in SoHo. I'd give my eyes, what's left of them, for her skin and hair. "How's the Great Escape going?"

"I flew the coop this morning. All my worldly possessions are locked up in that filing cabinet."

"No fooling," she says. "Congratulations."

The reality of what I've done suddenly scares me so much that I start to light another cigarette even though I've still got one burning in the ashtray.

"Nervous?"

"You could say that."

"I remember after I left Charlie I didn't have a regular period for six months. I also developed Irritable Bowel Syndrome and had to start seeing a psychiatrist."

"Jesus."

"But look at me now." She makes an expansive gesture that includes not just her well-functioning GI tract but her smart business suit (I come to work in jeans), silk blouse, eighty-dollar haircut and a hanging garden of costume jewelry on her wrists and fingers. "Estrogen helps."

"You're menopausal?"

"I had the whole deal—hot flashes, insomnia, night sweats. Plus the screaming meemies. I thank God every day for hormone replacement therapy. Even made my tits bigger. Of course, *you* won't have to worry about menopause for another ten years. By then they'll have probably figured out how to stop the aging process completely. If," she adds, "you don't kill yourself first with those things," nodding at my cancer sticks.

In ten years I'll be pushing fifty. In ten years I'll be ten years separated from my husband. Divorced. Going out of my mind with menopause. Will I have a man, any man, in my life?

"I actually only smoke when I'm around someone else who's smoking," I say. But my eyes have filled up at the thought of the lonely old age that's facing me. Dried up and undesirable. My ass flat and droopy, my boobs hanging down around my knees. I'm already homeless. Kevin's bed, where I've been sleeping ever since he went away to college, will be given to charity. The rest of my clothing and jewelry, all that I couldn't sneak out, will end up in a thrift shop. I'm just one step away from being one of those women who live in armories and wander the streets by day with all their belongings in a cart.

"Hey, kid. It's gonna be all right."

She somehow squeezes behind my desk and puts an arm around me. She smells like a high-class whore. I want to ask where she buys her perfume.

"Sorry," I say. "It just hit me. What I've gone and done."

"And a good thing too. If you thought too much beforehand you might never have managed it. I felt the same way after I left the jerk I was married to. But," she says, returning to the black fiberglass client's chair for another pull on my Marlboro, "look at me now."

After she leaves I try Harry's number, but there's no answer. I have two junkies scheduled to see me, but the first isn't due for almost an hour. This job is a joke. I didn't break my ass getting a high school diploma and then a college degree and masters, all with a young child to look after, to end up in a make-work gig in a smelly methadone clinic. I could have been a professional, a lawyer like my aunt Rose, though Rose wasted her life looking after a kosher widower and his graceless sons. I've already pissed away fifteen years in dead-end jobs just to keep some money coming in on a regular basis—my husband hasn't had a steady teaching job, any job at all, for the better part of a decade. But now it's my turn, I tell myself. No more living in terror of his anger or lust. I'm free, my own woman at last, I think, trying my boyfriend's number again in case he was only in the john when I called a few minutes ago. "Shit," I say when there's still no answer. "Shit, shit, shit."

Friday, December 19

I'm in my unpadded cell in the Tudor Arms, a "residence for professional ladies," the yellowed card on the dresser unsmirkingly calls it, just around the corner from Bloomindales and Henri Bendel. The room is ten by eight, slightly larger than a cell in Sing Sing. There's a common toilet and showers at the end of the hall. The walls are dirty orange, with a faded print of a farmhouse and horse over the bed instead of the crucifix that seems to belong there. On the floor is a gray rug worn down to the fiber where hundreds of professional ladies have laid their bare feet each morning before sallying forth to earn their bread. Besides the chest of drawers there's a small desk (professional ladies write a lot of letters, keep detailed accounts of their expenses, etc.) and a Bible. Professional ladies also keep diaries, as I apparently have begun to do in this marble-cover composition book that's identical to the one I used all through elementary school.

A telephone is provided on a fee-for-use basis. I use it to call Harry and masturbate while he tells me about his day at the office. I also masturbate between calls, while I'm reading one of my thrillers, waiting to go to sleep or waking up in the morning. I even masturbate when I'm with Harry, though not so as he notices, when he's in the shower or asleep. I've always masturbated, even as a young child. It takes my mind off things, the nasty things of life that won't go away.

Harry's loaned me his radio and I listen to talk shows or the news, it doesn't matter, as long as I can hear someone talking. My wardrobe is limited. Most of it is at Harry's. I take what I need there for the next couple days and bring back what I've worn to get cleaned. I wouldn't leave so much as a pair of pantyhose unattended in the Tudor Arms. The professional ladies I've seen in the hallways look like they wouldn't think twice about relieving a colleague of an unguarded toothbrush, never mind a genuine article of apparel.

Sometimes I wander over to Bloomie's to see what other women are wearing, especially the Puerto Rican salesgirls who always seem to be one fashion step ahead of everyone else. Or I take my thriller to the coffee shop on Lexington Avenue.

It's just occurred to me, what this room reminds me of—the camp my parents sent me to when I was nine. Freezing cabins, smelly toilets, silly girls and sadistic counselors. They made me play sports, softball, tennis, early-morning swims in the icy lake. I've had an aversion to anything athletic ever since, and my hand-eye coordination is still zilch. At home I broke so many plates my mother stopped asking me to wash dishes. After I got married my husband did virtually all the cooking.

I had to stand up to my husband to defend Kevin's decision not to go away to camp, one of the few times I've had the nerve to cross his father. I made other attempts to protect him from his father's bullying, but the boy's eventual breakdown shows how miserably I failed. My husband's mother spent her last years in a sanitarium, so Kev's condition is not entirely my fault. Even so, telling him that I've left his father is one of the hardest things I've ever had to do.

"You know how he is," I say when I finally worked up the nerve to call. "I stood it as long as I did partly for your sake, until I saw you were on your feet and able to manage. Even then I put it off for two more years out of pure cowardice."

Silence on the other end of the line. This was what I dreaded most, that he'd clam up like he did when his father used to browbeat him about not cleaning up his room exactly as he'd been told to, or was denying him supper until he had read a text out of the Bible about respect for legitimate authority. The boy would sit and rock, hour after hour, not responding to my attempts to comfort him, going stiff when I tried to hug or kiss him.

Only, now he was five hundred miles away and I couldn't even see him, much less try to touch him. "Please say something, Kev. Anything." Never mind if I go down the tubes myself, I thought. That's my own choice and I'm a big girl, however I may feel inside. But if my bolt for freedom causes my son a relapse, I'll never forgive myself.

"I know this is very upsetting for you," I said. "It's pretty upsetting for me too. Don't think I haven't thought long and hard before I did what I did. And not just about myself. I even worried how it would affect your father, though I don't think he'll feel anything like that kind of concern about me. He's a very disturbed man, Kev. Worse than you were even, because he doesn't realize it. Or refuses to. You and I were his co-dependents. To have a Tim Davis you need a Deirdre and a Kevin. But deep down he's like the Wizard of Oz, all *sturm* and *drang* with nothing but a scared little man behind the curtain. That's how bullies are. But even though I can see him now for what he is, up close I couldn't deal with him at all. Every time he thundered at me I felt like the Cowardly Lion."

I thought I heard something on the other end of the line. A sob? A giggle? Please God, I prayed, don't let him come apart on me. Give him the strength to bear this.

"Do you remember the time you took me and Allie Schwartz to see that movie?" he said. "Do you remember how Allie hid under the seat when the Wizard's face came on the screen?"

I tried not to let tears of relief overcome me. But I couldn't help myself.

"It's okay, Ma. We'll look out for each other."

Monday, December XX

There's no real mirror in the small foul toilet reserved for staff use. Just a piece of reflective metal over a dirty soapless sink. This used to be a clients' toilet, I'm told, until they started using it to shoot up or snort the stuff they purchase while waiting on line for their daily dose. I guess a mirror made of real glass can be made into a weapon of some kind.

I barely recognize myself in the dull gray reflection. Maybe it's just as well, I think as I apply lipstick to the area where my mouth should be. Better I shouldn't see what I look like after my first full week of freedom. So far I've spent every night with Harry because it's been too late for me to travel back to Manhattan on the subway and I can't afford to take a car service anymore. I'm still hoping he'll say, "Why not move in with me?" But Harry's newly divorced himself and leery about shacking up with someone who's only been separated from her own spouse barely a week. He says our lovemaking is the best he's ever had. I've learned a few trick over the years, muscular control and such, but mostly it's that I can't get enough of him and he feels it. A woman runs a risk when she exposes her sexual appetite like that to a man, but I've never been able to play the game of catch-me-if-you-can, not when I was sixteen and not now.

A light tapping on the toilet's door makes me shove my lipstick right into my nose. All I can do now is wipe it all off and start over.

"You've got a visitor," an unfamiliar voice says. But then I realize it's not so much unfamiliar as out of place.

"Connie?" I say, opening the door a few inches.

"Sorry to disturb you," she says, her high brown brow creased with apprehension. "I told him you weren't here. I said you were gone for the day. But he said, that's okay, he'll wait. I figured you'd want to know."

"Thanks," I say. "You're a brick."

"I'll call you when he leaves."

I dash back to my office and shut the door. There's no way for me to exit the building through anything but the main entrance without setting off a fire alarm and causing a general evacuation. Even so, I'm contemplating doing just that when a knock on the door puts my bowels into seizure.

"Who?" I call, praying it's just Laura or my supervisor or a homicidal junkie.

I watch the steel knob turn with the kind of helpless dread I feel at horror movies. And sure enough it's him: Godzilla, the Thing from Outer Space, Robert Redford, all rolled into one. His glasses are folded into the pocket of the plaid shirt I gave him last Christmas. His cheeks show a two-day growth of beard, but on him it doesn't look bad.

"May I?" he says as if he's just another client hoping for a referral to the local McDonald's.

He looks around the tiny office in the proprietary way all men view their physical surroundings, as if the world and everything in it were their birthright from Adam.

"I see what you mean," he says, referring to something I said several months back about my office being bigger than a bread box but smaller than a decent-size closet. He doesn't interrupt his inspection of the premises to see if I catch the reference because of course I do.

The phone rings and I grab it like it's something in motion.

"It's me, honey. Is he up there?"

"Sure is."

"You want me to tell Trevor to ask him to leave?"

I want him out of here, but I don't want to cause any more commotion than is necessary. "Give me five minutes."

"I won't keep you," he says, filling up the room so completely that there doesn't seem to be enough air for me to breathe. "I only came by to tell you that I miss you."

He reaches toward my hand which is still poised over the telephone as if to make sure the instrument doesn't slip away on me. I'm too petrified, or moved—I can't tell which at this point—to resist. His flesh comes to rest on my own. It's very warm, or mine is very cold, that hand that knows parts of my body better than I do myself, the hand which when my own was cupped safely inside used to make me feel that nothing bad, absolutely no harm could ever come to me as long as I remained joined to it.

"And I mean that," he says.

I expected a scene, recriminations.

I try to smile, afraid to say anything that might seem encouraging. I'd forgot how sweet he could be, how his touch went straight through me like a current even when he was at his worst and I hated him like I've never hated any other human being. This is why I had to sneak away instead of telling him to his face that I've had enough of his crazy personality. This is why I had to pretend that it was fear of his physical strength that I feared (he once locked me in my room for an entire afternoon) when what I really was afraid was he would ask me to stay, to not abandon him. He would say he needed me.

The phone rings again.

"You okay, honey?"

He raises his hand in the peace sign. "I'm leaving."

He's just a blur now, but I manage to hang on until he disappears entirely.

I'm shaking so bad I bite my lip. I can't even get a cigarette lit.

I turn away to avoid vomiting on my desk top but it's all dry retch. When it passes I reach for my Marlboros and smoke two, one right after the other. I try to stand, but my legs won't support me. I try again and manage to make it to the toilet. I sit down on the black seat I ordinarily never use without first lining it with clean toilet paper. I sit shitting and crying at the same time. And now I'm laughing as well.

"You okay in there?" Connie calls.

"Just swell," I say. "Never been better."

I laugh harder and Connie starts to jiggle the doorknob.

"Really," I say, "I'm okay."

I start to sing "We Shall Overcome," then realize it might sound disrespectful. I switch to "Bridge Over Troubled Water," but that only cracks me up again. Finally I flush, put myself in some kind of order and open the door. Connie is standing there just like my mother used to when I was constipated or had cramps and sat crying on the john while my father kept asking when was he going to get to use the bathroom. Connie doesn't look anything like my mother, but I enter her embrace willingly, let her nestle me in her big breasts, rocking back and forth. Like Ethel Waters and Shirley Temple, I think. Like Mary and the Christchild. Like a tree standing by the water.

III

Not Me

Tuesday, December 23

This is from a letter I received yesterday from my husband. There's no salutation, no date even. He sent it to my work address.

'Do you realize I have no way of paying January's rent? Is that what you want, for me to be evicted from the home where we've lived as man and wife for the last fifteen years? We raised our son here. Most of our friends still live in this neighborhood.

'You said in your letter that our relationship has become meaningless. You said that you live in fear and loathing of me.' [I actually wrote, "I live in a constant state of fear and anxiety"] 'If that's true I regret it. I never meant to make you afraid of me and never for one moment have I intended to do you any harm. I think you only bring these charges against me in order to justify your own selfishness. You took solemn vows before God' [We got married in city hall] 'to abide with me for better or for worse, in sickness and in health. You'll have to answer some day for turning your back on those vows....'

It gets worse. By the second page he's calling me a "shameless whore" (he would pronounce it "hoor"), a vicious woman who drove her only child to insanity. I'm used to his abuse. Only, of course I'm not. You never get used to abuse. I didn't even think of it as such until my boyfriend Harry used the word. We were lying in the bed he's fashioned out of pieces of timber left over from the bed frame he and his ex used to sleep on. I was telling him about the time my husband wouldn't let our son have his supper until he had read St. Paul's First Epistle to the Corinthians. Kevin has my stubbornness but he's just as terrified of his father as I am. So he chose to remain in his room, the one I moved into after he went away to college, rocking back and forth. Even after his father lifted his fatwa the boy refused to eat for two days.

"That's mental abuse," Harry said, looking like a crazy prophet in his bearded nakedness.

"No fooling," I said, but it was actually the first time I thought of Tim Davis as a spousal abuser. Till then I figured that's just how he is, a consequence of his own father's stern childraising combined with a touch of his mother's schizophrenia. I never thought to label his behavior at all. I just wanted to get away from it and felt awful because I couldn't protect my child from its worst excesses.

Of course, he wasn't abusive all the time. He could be very funny when he chose, and I love a good laugh more than anything. He would dress up as someone in the news, Yassir Arafat or Margaret Thatcher, and put me and Kevin into stitches. It's no wonder he was such a hit with his students, especially the females.

He's also written a letter to my mother. She's been living in Florida the last twenty years, the first ten with my father and, since Daddy's death, alone in a cinderblock shack in South Beach. She stayed on in New York just long enough to see her only grandchild into first grade, then let her husband talk her into moving to the geriatric promised land. Of course, it's changed radically down there. She doesn't dare open her door to a stranger and never goes out at night unless her friend Shelly picks her up.

She sent me the letter Tim Davis wrote her:

'I hold you responsible, Sybil, for the way your daughter has behaved. If you had raised her properly she would understand that marriage is a sacred trust not to be betrayed for mere personal convenience. "Let no man put asunder..."'

You can imagine how that goes down with a woman who has spent most of her adult life avoiding the holy-rollers of her own religion, only to have someone like Tim Davis quote the New Testament at her.

"End it," she told me the other night when I was looking for some maternal support.

"What do you think I'm trying to do?"

"I'm too old to have to deal with this sort of thing."

"Believe me, Mother, if there were some way I could spare you, I would. But you know how he is."

When she was younger and Tim Davis wasn't quite so crazy, she didn't mind his attentions one bit. My father was no match for her intellectually. Until my husband came into her life she got all her mental stimulation in the Russian Tea Room or at one of the other watering holes where her artistic friends gathered. As a young woman she studied in Paris and later worked on set design for the original *Porgy and Bess*. Why she married my father, a jobber in the fur trade who never graduated high school, will always be a mystery to me. Before I met Tim Davis I used to have fantasies about what life would have been like if I had been the daughter of the French art critic she made coy illusions to during our talks about her days at the Sorbonne. Instead of growing up in a building full of coarse Jews who made their livings in the Garment District, I would have had writers and painters for neighbors. I would have attended an *école supérieure* instead of Junior High School 239, a *lycée* instead of the Bronx High School of Science.

"Just end it," she says, having no more patience for my problems now than she did when I was sixteen. I tell myself to make allowances for her age, but the old resentment endures. She wasn't there for me when I had to face the shame of expulsion from high school, and she has no intention of being here for me now, at least not beyond mouthing the usual platitudes.

I tell her I'll call her next week at the usual time, then pull on some jeans to go out for coffee.

The elevator at the hotel where I'm staying is small and dark and reminds me of the one in the building on 121st Street. It stops at the third floor, but the door fails to open until I hit the Open Door button. Anyone who's lived in this rat trap for more than one day knows that on some floors it requires someone being on the inside of the elevator in order to get the door to open. It does no good complaining to the fat eunuch at the front desk. He either doesn't care or is too dimwitted to know what to do about it.

"Thank you, my dear, so much," a tiny old woman says as steps carefully over the gap between the elevator floor and the frame of the third-floor landing. Safely inside, she gives me a Clara Bow smile, her lips cherry-Jello red, her cheeks two brilliant but mismatched sunsets. If it wasn't for her advanced years—she looks easily twice my age—she might give some perverse meaning to this flophouse's motto.

"Going shopping," she says, patting the ancient knit bag she clutches to her chest like a sick cat.

I smile down at her (I'm barely five-three) and say she's picked the right neighborhood.

"I buy everything," she says, "in Henri Bendel. Ever since I was a girl," pronouncing "girl" as if it were a kind of nor'easter.

"Don't care for Bloomie's, do you?"

"Dear me, no. Not," she says, giving me a look like someone just passed wind, "my class of people."

I think: This could be me some day. Then I think: I should be so lucky. This old broad has an independent income. All I can count on when I hit sixty-five is a miserable Social Security check.

Even though it's not yet Thanksgiving, there are Christmas decorations up and down Lexington Avenue. It used to be that no one dared put up holiday lights until well into December. I hate Christmas. It follows you around the city like a crazy drunk, in and out of every building. Already they're playing carols on the Muzak in supermarkets. I feel like some kind of infidel, like I'm wearing a Star of David on my chest—an overreaction, since I usually don't feel any more Jewish than I do Christian. Harry knows more Yiddish than I do, and he's a Quaker.

I sit down in the last empty booth in the coffee shop near 58th Street where I sometimes have breakfast. The Greek at the register gives me a look, but I figure I spend enough money here to rate a booth to myself on a weekday afternoon. I open my thriller and order a piece of pie and coffee. The waitress is the only one in the place who speaks English. I like her because she has a big birthmark

on her left cheek and doesn't try to cover it up with makeup and because the men who work here, all Greeks, treat her like a dog.

I take my husband's letter out of my bag and start to read again:

'We've been part of each other ever since that day we fooled
around in the stairwell outside the chemistry lab. You've seen me
through some tough years, and don't think I don't appreciate it. You
had some tough years yourself, having to look after Kev while finish-
ing your schooling at night. I'm the first to applaud you.

'But I made sacrifices too. You weren't always there for me when
I came home from work and you had to run right out to your classes. And later, when you started working yourself, your career always
came first. Your career has always come first, and it's been me and
our child who paid the price for that. I know you hold me responsible for the women I consorted with, but maybe if you had been
home more often I wouldn't have been tempted. My past behavior is
no excuse for what you're doing to me now....'

It's vintage Tim Davis—the sweetness, the paranoia, the com-
pulsive accusation. He can melt you one moment with gentleness
and humor, and the next he's calling you vile names. I blink the tears
out of my eyes as the waitress brings my pie and coffee.

"Okay?" she says.

"Okay," I say, grateful for a stranger's compassion in this cold
city at this most cheerless time of the year.

Outside, the sidewalk is crowded with shoppers and street traffic is gridlocked, most of it Yellow cabs. A Salvation Army Santa is
swinging a bell near the corner of 59th Street, his red suit hanging so
slack that he looks like he hasn't had a good meal himself since last
Christmas.

We stopped putting up a tree after Kevin moved out. My husband said the Christmas tree is a pagan tradition that has nothing to
do with the birth of Jesus. I guess that's why my mother and father
always had one, and they didn't pretend it was a Chanukah Bush. In
any case, I've always considered Christmas trees, like everything else
associated with this holiday, a dumb idea. I enjoy a good performance
of Handel's *Messiah*, though, especially "I Know that My Redeemer
Liveth." I used to ask my husband to take me to performances in
churches on the Upper West Side. Later I started going by myself.

The last couple years I stayed home and listened on the radio. Bach is my favorite composer, but Handel is no slouch.

'This will be the first Christmas we've spent apart in twenty-five years.' [He's counting the two years before I had Kevin] 'We haven't made much of the holidays since Kev moved out, but our spending them together has always meant a great deal to me, even if all we do is cook a turkey or put a wreath on the door. This Christmas will be a very lonely one for me.'

I'm crying again, not blubbering like I still do sometimes when I'm alone but leaking tears like a faucet that needs a new washer, like the one in our bathroom that my husband has been saying for the past two years he'll fix this week for sure.

It's pure bull, that business about us keeping Christmas together. Last year he wouldn't let me out of the kitchen until he had read me all four evangelists' accounts of the birth of Jesus and then gave an exegesis on the apparent discrepancies between each. His Jewish mother, my husband's I mean, would have seen the lunacy in that, crazy as she was herself.

"I'm not interested in the birth of Jesus," I said, knowing better than to try to force my way past him. "It's all just a marketing scheme, a way for business to make money. May I please go now?"

"The birth of Christ is the seminal moment in the history of Western civilization. You're a member of that civilization, however much you may deny it."

"I'm a Jew from the Bronx, and a half-assed Jew at that, as you're fond of pointing out."

"Christ was a Jew. Christianity was a Jewish sect for its first hundred years."

"That's very interesting, but can I please go to the john? My bladder is bursting." What I actually had was menstrual cramps, but he wouldn't consider those a valid reason for interrupting his diatribe.

"As a Jew, you represent the seedbed out of which Western culture arose."

"What about the Greeks? What about the Romans?"

I couldn't care less about the Greeks and Romans—or the bloody Jews, for that matter. I just wanted out of that kitchen.

"I'm talking about the historical premise upon which all subsequent cultural evolution took place: the Paulite idea of a divine, redemptive incarnation intended for the spiritual rehabilitation of all men."

He wasn't so much talking as writing now, whipping up a little monograph while I sat trapped behind the kitchen table, refusing to double up in agony as I felt like doing. He no longer does any work in his own field. All his intellectual energies—and they once were considerable—now go into this religious crap. He used to hang out with the Berrigans until they got tired of his telling them they didn't understand the true meaning of Christ's message. Now he votes straight Republican and refuses to go to mass unless it's in Latin.

"I'm talking," he went on, "about the existential locus of mankind's deepest spiritual longings," placing his hands on the kitchen table as though it were a lecturn. His face was alive in a way that it rarely is anymore except when he's holding forth about Jesus or St. Paul. He used to look like that, not quite so manic, when he talked about Milton and Sartre. My heart ached almost as much as my womb to see him reduced to the narrow-minded bully he'd become.

"Could I *please* go to the john? Before I pee on the floor?"

"'Saul, Saul,'" he said, leaning across the table where half a piece of cold toast lay in a chipped blue saucer that was the last remaining piece of our wedding set, "'why dost thou persecute me?'"

A Yellow cab makes a sudden stop just outside the coffee shop where I'm still nursing my pie and coffee. The cab behind it, never more than a few feet away, slams into its trunk. I used to hear the same loud thud when I was lying in Kevin's old bed, waiting to fall asleep. It's not at all like the sound cars make when they crash in the movies or on television. Only when I saw a real accident happen— cabs then as well—did I realize what I had been hearing during those sleepless nights.

The driver of the first cab, a Sikh in a light blue turban, has gotten out of his vehicle and is inspecting the damage. Meanwhile, the driver of the cab that has just plowed into him, a Russian émigré is my guess, is shouting and waving his arms as if this were the Nevsky Prospect. A cop suddenly appears, takes out that long black notebook cops carry and begins to calmly write something in it. Meanwhile,

Sasha continues to declaim at Mr. Singh, who looks as though he has four kids and a pregnant wife to support. Only one pedestrian, a homeless black man with a full shopping bag in each hand, stops to watch.

I take out from my Coach bag a carefully folded sheet of white typing paper. Then I root around until I locate a leaky ballpoint.

"Dear Tim," I begin. I think about including the date (though no return address, of course), but decide against it, thinking that what I'm about to write should seem settled and not just the expression of one particular day or mood. But as soon as I think about him holding this piece of paper in his hand, my brain turns into day-old oatmeal. Deirdre Finley Davis, magna cum laude graduate of CCNY, author of a masters thesis singled out for "special remarks and appreciation," all achieved while caring full-time for a young child, suddenly can't put two words together. I want to tell him I'm sorry, that I truly regret it's come to this but that it's not all my fault, that he should take a good hard look at himself, give serious consideration to seeing a therapist—that I'd even help him pay for it. But after ten minutes of staring at the blank page all I've been able to produce is heartburn.

I walk down to 57th Street and head west, past Bonwit Teller's and Fortunoff and the little shop where I used to buy French turtle-necks (*"On reconnait toujours un vrai Corrigan"*). I looked great in them. Anyone would. Nowadays I'm lucky if I can afford one good piece of clothing a year.

When I was little my mother took me on shopping expeditions to fancy stores like Lord & Taylor as well as to little holes-in-the-wall that never advertised in the *Times*, rarely even hung a sign outside. You reached their showrooms by small, slow elevators and paid in cash unless you were a regular customer. Ill-lit places staffed by one or two middle-aged Jewish men who didn't seem to care one way or the other if you bought anything, an attitude I put down to in-bred cynicism until I was old enough to understand that anyone who made the effort to seek out that kind of establishment didn't need high-pressure sales tactics.

She bought all my own clothes in Altman or Macy's. She would've taken the same time and expense with what I wore as she did with her own exquisite wardrobe, but I had no interest in clothing, even as a teenager.

I'm just crossing Madison Avenue when I run into, literally almost get knocked down by, Beth Wyman. Her husband is an assistant commissioner with the city. When Tim Davis was teaching at Fordham, the four of us used to spend a lot of time together. Ben was a dean then at Fordham's Lincoln Center campus and got free tickets to the Philharmonic and New York State Opera.

We both agree it's been ages, then she asks the inevitable question to which I have to decide pretty fast whether I tell her or don't tell her.

"Actually, Tim and I have split up," I say as pedestrians begin to elbow us out of the way. "Just last week, as a matter of fact."

She's delighted of course to pick up a piece of breaking news this juicy and suggests we go somewhere for a cup of tea. I never much liked Beth, though her husband's okay. She's always seemed more an attachment than a person, one of those women who are just show pieces for their successful spouses. She has a Larchmont-lock-jaw accent and gets herself depilated regularly. She took me to her salon once. I decided that women who go in for that sort of thing couldn't have very good sex lives.

We settle on a place at the corner of Sixth Avenue just down the block from the Russian Tea Room where my mother spent so many long afternoons with her artistic and musical friends while her half-blind husband was earning our keep in the dingy freight elevators and dusty cutting floors of Seventh Avenue.

"I'm so sorry," she says after we give the young Italian waiter our order. "Was this something sudden or has it been in the works for a while?"

She has a mauve silk scarf wrapped around her neck. Her hairdo must have cost a month's rent. But she seems genuinely dismayed by what I've told her, so I give a fuller account of my woes than I intended to. I guess I need someone to talk to, someone besides my boyfriend Harry.

"It's been in the cards for a while," I say. "Ever since Kevin went away to college. I actually moved out once before, just for a couple weeks. This time it's for keeps."

"Has it been that long since we last saw each other?"

"Daniel's graduation."

Her son Daniel is a Harvard graduate.

"Three years! We used to get together every weekend when Ben was working at Fordham."

"Time flies," I say. It was she who stopped asking us over when my husband went on unemployment after Fordham laid him off.

"I knew you and Tim had your problems, but I never imagined it would come to this. Is there no chance," she says as her overstuffed eclair arrives, "that you'll get back together?"

"Between slim and none."

She wipes her mouth carefully with a big red linen napkin. "Is there...someone else?"

I owe her nothing, not even information. She'll repeat anything I do tell her to her husband who may or may not decide to give Tim Davis a call. If he does, my husband will get out of him every word I've said to this preposterous woman. Even so, I oblige her. I'm through with subterfuge. I've lived by it for too many years. I tell her how Harry and I met, how horny I was, not for just any man but for someone like him, someone who cares what I think and feel, who asks me if I like Chinese food before he takes me to a Chinese restaurant. I tell her how good our sex is.

"Marvelous," she says, blushing as I hoped she would. "I wish you all the best, Deirdre, I really do. I had no idea your marriage was so dreadful."

"I have nobody but myself to blame. A bully needs a willing victim."

She stares at me as if I've just said I eat sanitary napkins. She clearly doesn't have a clue to who this woman is she was once friends with. I find her reaction immensely satisfying. I'm *not* that woman anymore.

"Here," I say, reaching for my Coach bag which she eyed with interest when we sat down. I smooth out my husband's letter on the table between us.

She watches through her mascara as if to say, 'What have I got myself into?' But I'm doing this for me, not for her.

"Dear, dear," she says putting on a pair of beige half-focals. She starts to read the first page, her cheeks glowing. It's an odd tribunal I've chosen to plead my case to but, I think, it may be the only one. Here ye, hear ye, in the matter of Deirdre Finley Davis vs. Timothy Michael Davis...

A moment later she abruptly removes her glasses and puts them back in her bag. Her hands are trembling. "Where does the time go?" She keeps her eyes lowered as she gathers her things together. "I'm so sorry," she says, on her feet now and reaching across the table to give my arm a squeeze. "Maybe we could...get together sometime. Call me when you're, you know, settled."

"Sure."

"I hate to rush off," she says pulling on foot-long calfskin gloves. "A dental appointment. I almost forgot." She manages a laugh, another squeeze of my arm, this time harder, and she's gone, vanished, poof.

The waiter asks would I like another pot of tea, but I say no thanks I've never much cared for tea as a matter of fact.

Outside it's begun to snow. Big, wet New York snow that melts on contact with the busy sidewalks. For snow to stick in this city it has to fall in the dead of night, sneaky as a thief. Weather is optional, a kind of tourist, something that only happens for real in Ohio or Colorado where they have nothing better to occupy them.

She's slept with him. That's why she turned red and left half a perfectly good eclair on her plate. That's why we stopped getting invited over—not because Tim Davis got laid off but because things had come to a head for them. He'd had enough of her, or she wanted him to leave me.

No chance. He'd hang on to me if he had a hundred women. Not because I'm something special but because that's how he is, how he's always been, even when we were teenagers. Not even because he loves me. Just because. Till one of us is dead for better or for worse.

The Italian waiter makes a sortie at my left flank to see if he can't move me along.

I actually did the right thing in leaving him, I think, fishing in my bag for a tip. A first for me. I feel like I've won something.

It's snowing like a son-of-a-bitch now, and the rush-hour traffic doesn't like it one bit. They blow horns at the snow. They curse it. But I walk toward the subway that will ferry me to my lover in Brooklyn, feeling like a princess in a fairy tale. The snow is my special friend. I wouldn't be surprised to see Bambi come skipping down 6th Avenue, though five'll get you ten he'd end up chopped meat before he got as far as Times Square.

But not me, I think as I drop two quarters into the kettle of a Santa shivering next to the entrance to the "F" train.

"Merry Christmas," he says.

"Likewise," I say, and then drop in the rest of the change I had taken out to buy a subway token. "You guys should strike for warmer suits."

"Tell me about it," he says. "Merry Christmas."

"Merry Christmas," I say, then beat it out of there before my ten-league boots turn into soggy marshmallows.

IV

Memory and Desire

Friday, December 27

Dear Lou-Ann,
I meant to write you sooner, but unavoidable circumstances etc., etc.
Tim and I have split up. Two weeks ago I removed the last of my stuff from
121ˢᵗ Street, the little that I dared sneak out in shopping bags one bag at a time
until I had filled up the filing cabinet in this cubbyhole of an office with my skirts
and slacks and shoes and jewelry and the few personal items I couldn't bear to
leave behind, such as the photographs of Kevin and Joshua taken when we were
all together out in Oregon.
Leaving Tim Davis is something I should have done a long time ago but just
didn't have the guts for. Why now, when I'm just a few weeks shy of my fortieth
birthday? Partly it has to do with the man I've been seeing, actually seeing quite
a lot of if you get my drift. Thanks to him I feel like maybe I have a right to a
real life after all, like maybe I don't have to put up with Tim's craziness forever
out of some sense of guilt or obligation. His name is Harry, by the way, my
boyfriend, lover, whatever. He works for the city, a social worker.
I really did intend to write you before, but somehow the days and weeks
passed in a kind of fog. Then one morning I woke up and realized that half
my life was shot to hell without any real prospect of things getting any better. I've
been in the same job for five years, a crummy counseling position ("Employment

Specialist") in a disgusting methadone clinic in Chinatown. The entire neighborhood reeks of fish and some kind of rancid cooking oil. My office is the size of a coffin and on a busy day I see maybe four clients. The rest of the time I read. I have nothing in common with any of the other people who work here, they're all wrapped up in their families and the latest movies. I don't have a real family of my own anymore, not since Kevin moved out. He's doing okay, by the way. The medication seems to have him stabilized, thank God.

Even so, I should have dropped you a line now and then. We were so close back when Alan and Tim were going for their masters at the University of Oregon....

Ten years is a long time to be out of touch from someone who was a close friend, not that I really expect to take up right where we left off. The last time I saw Lou-Ann she was living in an upscale neighborhood near San Francisco. I only met her second husband that one time and probably wouldn't recognize her children if I ran into them on the street.

In our early twenties we were inseparable, back when our husbands were classmates in the English department on Dowland Fellowships. We shopped, ate and even camped out together. She was the sister I never had. The *friend* I never had, before or since. It seems incredible I could let a relationship like that just lapse.

My mother is too old to be much of a friend to me. Not true—she's never really cared what was going on in my life, not when I got pregnant in my senior year of high school, not now when my marriage is finally breaking up. When I told her in a rare expression of my true feelings that my life seemed like a waste of time and resources that might be better spent on someone else, she said, "My darling Deirdre, you're a lovely young woman with your whole life ahead of you." I suppose if you're seventy-five that's how forty looks. More likely, she just didn't want to hear about my troubles, any more than she did twenty years ago.

Lou-Ann would care, but I'm not sure she would understand. It's not just a question of the time that's passed. She's been living a life that seems more alien to me than that of a bunch of tribesmen in Outer Mongolia. Her husband is a software executive and they live in a big house in the suburbs. The last time I visited they were planning to sell that house because they could get a better tax write-off on a bigger one in the same neighborhood. They have three cars, one of them a kind of truck I couldn't even get into without help. All she talked about the whole time I was there was her children and whether they would get into good colleges, and her job at an abortion clinic. She hates Pro-Lifers, takes them personally. I guess if I had to worry about being blown up every time I set foot into this rat hole I work in, I'd feel more sympathetic. I wish they *would* blow it up, but not when I'm inside.

It's ironic that she should be working in an abortion clinic (technically a "woman's health care facility"). Where was she when I needed her, when I was sixteen? Girls were getting abortions even then before it became legal, but I was too scared to go and find someone on my own, and my parents never even mentioned the possibility. I doubt I would have followed through, though, if they did. I was crazy about Tim Davis and he felt the same way about me.

...My life seems such a mess. If only I hadn't gotten pregnant. I had plans to go to law school. And look where I've ended up. I know there are plenty of people who have it a lot harder than I do, but I really should be doing better than this, Lou-Ann. I knocked myself out to get a college degree. I actually had to bring Kevin to class with me sometimes. He was such a good kid, half the time no one even noticed him. Getting my masters was a snap by comparison.

Back then you were like a sister to me....

But that ended when we moved back to New York. It was my idea, coming back east. I couldn't stand Oregon. Everyone talked so slow. There was no place to get a decent pizza, they didn't even know what a bagel was, much less have one to sell. I missed my mother. I missed the subway.

...This isn't the first time I've left Tim. Two years ago I took a room at the "Y." But then he went and broke his leg—some sort of boating accident with his friends out in the Hamptons. He said he would starve to death all alone in that apartment. Like a jerk I believed him. Not true: I wanted to believe him. He has a million friends, half of them female and under thirty. They would have been only too glad to stop by and boil him an egg and probably ream him out as

well. But I talked myself into believing he really needed me. The funny thing is, he does, but not to cook or look after him. He needs me in some way I don't quite understand but frightens me, because his need appeals to something in me I seem to have no control over. That's why I had to sneak out of that apartment the way I did, leaving most of my belongings behind and only doing so after Kevin was safely out on his own. That's why I'm wearing the same clothes every week to work and washing out my pantyhose in the communal sink of this "professional ladies residence" where I'm living....

I want to tell her how scared I am. Scared that Harry will get tired of me, scared that Tim Davis will find out where I'm living, even scared I'll lose my nerve and go back to him if he breaks another leg or gets sick. But I don't write any of this. Instead, I fold the letter and put it away in the back of my composition book. Then I lie down on the lumpy mattress (by now I'm back in my hotel room) and stare up at the water marks on the ceiling. Out in the hallway two women are arguing about who stole the other's soap from the shower.

I start to masturbate. Not because I'm horny, though I am, I always am, but just to take my mind off everything I don't want to think about. I think about Harry, how he smells when we're making love, that hard masculine smell that excites me so much when he's inside me but find unpleasant the rest of the time. Sometimes Harry turns into Tim Davis, a very young Tim Davis who smelled no different than I did, almost like a newborn, that sweet baby smell Kevin had. We used to do it every day and just about every place as well, in broom closets, on subway platforms—down at the very end where no one goes, though a few motormen must have got an eyeful—one time in a snowbank. I didn't even notice the cold, and I wear three layers of clothing even on a warm day and never sleep without two or more blankets.

His body seemed like an extension of my own. He was what I had been longing for every time I touched myself, and I can remember my mother telling me to stop touching myself even when I was a toddler. He had the parts I was so hungry for but didn't know it. I felt whole when he was with me, just like in that Greek myth about human beings being split in two parts and having to search for the halves they were separated from. I didn't need or want anyone but him. He was my all in all. It's corny to put it that way, but that's how it was.

There was romance too, only I would have called it "loyalty." He stuck by me, and that was worth more than any flowers or boxes of chocolate (Harry buys me a present almost every day and I love him for it, so I guess I've changed). When my parents got wind that we were having sex they sent me away to a summer camp upstate. The camp directors intercepted Tim's letters, on my parents' orders, so he hopped a bus up to the little jerkwater town nearby. He sent me a postcard signed with my parents' names, adding some Latin at the bottom which the Jewish camp administrators would never understand. I ran away to the motel where he was staying and we fucked to beat the band, living off potato chips and Coke from a vending machine until the police came and arrested him for statutory rape (he was sixteen by then but I wasn't).

I refused to go back to the camp or to have anything to do with the court case. I told my parents they had better arrest me too, because I wasn't going back to New York unless they dropped the charges against Tim. My father threatened to put me in a "home," some kind of reform school, but I told him to go ahead, I didn't care and he'd never see me again for the rest of his life. He did drop the charges, but when Tim and I got caught doing it in the school gym that semester, my father had him arrested again and this time he meant business.

That was the worst time of my life, worse than being expelled, worse than anything I went through after I was married, and I went through plenty.

First was the court case. They forced me to testify. I refused to say anything against Tim, but I also wouldn't deny we were having sex because that would have meant that what we were doing was wrong, when it was the one right thing in my life. They gave Tim two years probation and ordered that I see a psychiatrist for not less than six months.

The shrink was a middle-aged Irish guy who wanted me to talk about my earliest memories, and I have excellent recall. He seemed as bored as I was, but once he found out I was a "chronic masturba-

tor" he perked up and wanted me to talk about virtually nothing else
and got red in the face the way the Irish do when they talk about sex.
I told my father the guy was playing with himself, and for once my
father took my side and said I didn't have to go back anymore, he
would deal with the judge himself if there was a problem about it.

Why am I writing all this down? Is it some kind of therapy or am
I afraid what might happen to me if things don't turn out the way I
hope they will? I've never kept a diary. Diaries were for blond shik-
sas, Nancy Drew types, with the obvious exception of Anne Frank,
but she was a foreigner. I don't expect anyone to read it. I don't *want*
anyone to. I think maybe I'm writing because next month I turn forty
and I feel like one of those polar explorers (I always wanted to be an
explorer, it was one of the few real ambitions I've ever had), like I
may not make it to my destination but feel obliged to record what's
happening right up to when the last candle is used up and the last
dog dies.

My obstetrician was my uncle, Aunt Bella's husband, my father's
sister, the one with the twitch, so technically he wasn't a blood relative—isn't, I mean, the bastard's still alive. The idea was to keep it in
the family. I thought I was just going for a consultation, but he gave
me a full internal. I didn't have the nerve to object, by then I was too
ashamed of myself, not for the condition I was in but because I had
lost control of my life and was being treated like a small child again.
I think he sexually molested me.

The labor and delivery were horrible. It seemed to go on forever.
At first they wouldn't let Tim Davis in to see me, so all I had for
company were some nasty nurses who thought the pain I was going through was just what I deserved. One of them, her name was
Fuchs, I'll never forget her, she actually said, "Maybe next time you'll
keep your legs together until you've got a husband." They told my
mother she had to stay outside in the waiting room and, wimp that
she was, she did.

By the time my water broke I was exhausted. But the labor went
on for another six hours. I was screaming for a painkiller, but Fuchs
or one of her sadistic sisters said my doctor hadn't left any order for
a painkiller, I'd have to wait till he got there. When he finally turned

up I told him he was a Nazi quack, he and the rest of them belonged in Auschwitz. He gave me an injection posthaste to shut me up. It was only long afterward that I realized how embarrassing it must have been for him, even if he did fool around with me on the examining table, the bastard.

...Why don't you come east for a couple weeks? I could take some time off from work and we could bum around like we used to do in Oregon. I could get tickets for a Broadway play or one of the better Off-Broadway productions. We could take in a couple concerts, hang out in the Village, go shopping. I'll bet you still love to shop. I'm only sorry you won't get to see Kevin. He was so fond of you when he was little. You were like an aunt to him....

    I sometimes wonder why I haven't made female friends like other women do, long-term friends. It seems I've always depended on the man in my life to be my best friend, my only friend. Even during the worst times with Tim Davis I looked on him as the one person who knew me well enough and long enough to give me advice, though what he usually did was lecture me about right and wrong, and guess which of those I was. Now I look to Harry. He's a social worker, listening and giving advice come naturally to him.

    My husband wasn't always such a moralist. In his youth he was a big iconoclast, an anti-cleric even. That was also when he was screwing everything in a skirt, though to be fair young women threw themselves at him, and not just his students, practically every woman on the street. They literally followed him around. At first I was flattered to be married to a man that attractive, but when I found out he was sleeping with most of them, my attitude changed in a hurry, not toward him but toward myself. I began to feel ugly and uninteresting. Lou-Ann tried to perk me up, get me to buy new clothes instead of schlepping around in the same baggy jeans all the time. But I refused. I was stupid, I said that if my husband couldn't love me for who I was, why should I demean myself by trying to compete with the butt-twitchers who were chasing him around campus? Inside, though, I felt that if I were him I'd do just what he was doing. I wouldn't want to be saddled with a wife and child when other young men were still having a good time for themselves.

I used to take long drives out to the coast. I'd wait till my husband was asleep for the night, then get in our old Ford—the only car we ever owned—and drive as far and as fast as I dared. It rains all the time in Oregon, so I didn't do it for the scenery. I did it for the sense of control and escape, and for the danger, the roads were always wet and not very well lit. When I reached the Pacific I turned around and drove straight back. I didn't have any hanky-panky in mind, that came much later. All I wanted was to get away, to feel the speed of the road beneath me.

I would get home just as the sky was growing light. Tim didn't even know I had gone anywhere. If he woke up and found me missing from the bed beside him, he assumed I was downstairs, reading. I lay beside him until the alarm went off, then pretended to be asleep. He'd bring Kevin in to me before he left for his classes, and that was when I slept. God knows how the boy survived on his own in that big house. He could easily have stuck something into an electrical outlet or turned on the stove and burned the place down.

...Do you remember Sal Galasano? He was a Dowland Fellow, I met him at the reception for incoming grad students. He was on the public-TV news show the other night. He works for one of those Washington think tanks, conservative of course. He's lost all his hair and looks to be about thirty pounds heavier than when we knew him. Otherwise he looks exactly the same as he did twenty years ago....

Actually, Lou-Ann probably wouldn't remember Sal Galasano, her husband didn't mix much with other Dowland Fellows except for Tim. Sal came up to me at the reception for incoming students. He thought I was there on a fellowship too, but I didn't realize that right away. I thought he was just being friendly. He asked where I had gone to college and seemed impressed when I said CCNY. He was short, barrel-shaped, reminded me of Marty, especially after he told me he was from the Arthur Avenue section of the Bronx just like the character in the Paddy Chayefsky play. He had gone to Fordham College, practically right across the street. I finished up my high school nights at Theodore Roosevelt on Fordham Road, so we had something to chat about for a while, until Tim Davis spotted us and decided to tear himself away from whatever female had attached herself to him. I introduced Sal, I remember how surprised he looked when I referred to Tim Davis as my husband, he turned quite red.

It was one of the few times I can ever remember my husband getting jealous, and I didn't even realize that was what it was until several years later—until quite recently, actually. I couldn't imagine anyone, least of all Tim Davis, feeling jealous because of me. I used to get an upset stomach when a salesgirl smiled at him, never mind what he got up to with his students. I considered myself lucky that he went on living with me. I was terrified he'd leave Kevin and me and I'd have to go through the rest of my life alone and unloved. I didn't believe for a moment anyone else could care for me, which probably explains why I eventually went with the kind of men I did.

Men like Forrest. His real name, by the way. He was my first WASP, my first and only. It was partly his name that attracted me, that and the way he was dying to get into my pants. Nobody ever pursued me like that, not even Tim Davis, because with him the feeling had been mutual, I wanted Tim as much as he wanted me.

God knows Forrest didn't have much else going for him. He was everything Tim Davis was not or, more accurately, he had absolutely nothing to recommend him by comparison. He wasn't ugly, but he was no Cary Grant and had at best an ordinary intelligence, no interest in books or art. His name was the only thing classy about him, his family were working-class. What overcame all these shortcomings was his single-minded appetite for my snatch.

I'm not very proud of that period of my life. Our "affair" lasted almost a decade. All during that time Tim Davis and I went on living as man and wife, only now I had someone to turn to when my husband was chasing his butt-twitchers.

...How about giving serious consideration to taking a trip to New York? I've been looking at one-bedroom apartments. You could stay with me as long as you like. I've missed you, Lou-Ann, we should never have lost touch the way we did.

V

Open Spaces

Friday, January 28

I've found an apartment I can afford. It's on the West Side, in Chelsea, way over on 9th Avenue but just one long block from the IND train. I can change at West 4th for the "F," and then it's just a few stops to East Broadway where I work.

I moved in last weekend without a stick of furniture, with not much more than the clothes I was wearing, the rest are still at my boyfriend Harry's in Brooklyn. I bought an air mattress to sleep on. Anything is better than spending another night in the Tudor Arms, I can't believe I lasted five weeks there. I won't change my address officially for a while, though, in case my husband tries to find me. It's bad enough he knows where I work.

I still can't believe I found an apartment so quickly. People spend months looking and then end up having to share with someone, the rents are so outrageous. I just walked in off the street, rang the super's bell and asked if there was anything available. He said there was a one-bedroom, would I like to see it—all this over the intercom. I said, sure, I'll look at it, and he said he'd be right up to show it to me.

He didn't introduce himself and neither did I, so I knew I was dealing with a real New Yorker.

"Elevator's over here," he said, and good thing he did because the lobby was dark, coming right in off the street. I didn't even have a chance to get a look at him. "It's slow, but it gets you there." I felt at home, like I did for the better part of the twenty years I lived with my husband and son on the Upper West Side or when I was growing up on Tremont Avenue in the Bronx, though the supers then were always black or Puerto Rican, the only dark faces you'd see in those buildings thirty, forty years ago.

He's a nice-looking fellow, the super, early-forties I'd guess. Probably Irish, I'd give my eye teeth for their skin. He didn't say anything else till we reached the third floor and the elevator doors groaned open. "This way." I followed him down a gray but clean hallway to 3F, and he started fishing through the big key chain on his hip. The door opened with the first key he tried.

He pushed open the door and waited for me to enter. Very few men have held a door for me. Certainly not my husband. Not the man I went with for ten years. Not anyone I can think of except the odd stranger...and Harry, of course. Harry is always holding doors and taking my arm when we cross streets, though I guess it should actually be me taking his, only I've never taken a man's arm in my life and would feel silly starting now.

"It's bright. It's clean," he said, taking a stroll around the big living room as if he were a real estate agent. He checked the radiator, tested the window locks. There are several windows. The view is of 9th Avenue—westerly. "You might want to put up a window gate on the fire escape exit. I have one in the basement you could have."

I said I'd like that, partly because I hadn't said anything at all except hello when we were still in the building's outer vestibule. I still didn't know what the rent was, so I asked. When he told me I was so relieved I started talking a mile a minute, and I'm a very close-mouthed person ordinarily, ask anyone.

I checked out the kitchen. It was sunny, had plenty of cabinets and room enough for a small table. Then I started opening closets, you can never have too many of those, all the while running my mouth like someone on speed. I can't even remember what I said, except that it was about how hard it is to find an affordable place to live and how happy I was I had done so. He said nothing himself, just went on checking and testing things—windows, stove, light switches--as if he had encountered this reaction before, like those people who hand out turkeys to poor people at Thanksgiving.

I had already said, "I'll take it," and was on my way out when I suddenly realized something.

"Where's the bedroom?"

He let the door swing gently closed again as if he knew I was going to ask this question, like a doctor who's been explaining how a particular medical procedure will be performed knows you're eventually going to eventually remember to ask, "But how will I be able to function if you remove most of my brain?"

"It's what they call a one-and-a-half," he said, with no indication whether he approved or disapproved of the designation. He was all professional.

I looked again at the big L-shaped room. I had assumed the shorter part of the "L" was a dining area.

"Most people use a sofa-bed," he said. "It's for a single person—an individual, I mean."

He pulled open the door again. "Still interested?"

Just then the late afternoon sun came out from behind a cloud and flooded the apartment with golden light. The apartment on 121st Street faced north, and my room in the Tudor Arms had no window at all.

"I'll take it."

He invited me to go down to his office to fill out an application. He got chatty in the elevator, about as chatty as he probably ever gets.

"Most of the tenants are working people. It's a quiet building," he said.

The elevator doors opened onto a big basement space with an overhead of thick insulated pipes. Everything was painted white except for the concrete floor which was dark gray. A boiler rumbled like a big ship's engine.

"This way."

My job as Employment Specialist sometimes takes me into factories and machine shops, even more so the job I had before this when I worked for an agency that was supposed to help ex-cons find work. I usually don't think twice about sitting down in a dark corner with some rough manager of an assembly plant much gloomier than this one, it's just part of my job. Every so often one of them tries to cop a feel, but I've developed a set response that usually puts the situation back on a strictly business basis: "Mr. X, I'm willing to pretend that didn't happen and get back to the real reason why I'm here. Or, I can leave and ask my agency to send someone else to conduct this interview." It usually works, though a couple times I've had to wrestle my way out of a literally tight spot with some octopus in a greasy shirt and garlic on his breath.

The super—his name is Cleary, I had to ask—didn't give the least indication of having anything but business on his mind, and he isn't bad looking, he could probably get over with some women. His "office" is a room right next to the boiler which, besides his desk and swivel chair and a worn but still serviceable straight-backed wooden chair for guests like myself, houses the tools of his trade, everything from a snow-blower to a full set of hand wrenches, a locked cabinet for duplicate tenants' keys, a small TV, calendar (snow scene—I've seen some doozies) and an answering machine. There are also a couple items I wasn't used to finding in this sort of setting—a bookshelf containing manuals for boiler and electrical maintenance alongside *Typhoon* and *The Nigger of the Narcissus.*

He gave me a standard lease to sign in triplicate, explaining that it wouldn't be executed until the landlord verified the information on my application. I asked how soon I could move in. He said as soon as the application was approved, in a few days, a week at most.

"In the meantime, I'll tighten up the screws on the kitchen cabinets"—I hadn't noticed they were loose—"and put up that window gate. If you need to get in touch with me," he said, pulling a thick white lined pad to within writing range as the boiler kicked on with a roar, "I'm available at this number until five o'clock." He scratched out seven digits in a large, bold hand and ripped the sheet from the pad. "And in case you need to reach me for an emergency, this is my home number," adding a second set of digits with the same exchange as the first. "If I'm not there, my wife will be. And you can always leave a message on the answering machine here in the office."

I moved in that weekend. Harry brought some Chinese takeout and helped inflate my air mattress. Then he did the same for me, a kind of house blessing. Afterward we lay looking up at a big pink moon over 9th Avenue.

"You have to get furniture," he said.

"I kind of like it like this. Nothing to clean. Just sweep up the takeout cartons every couple weeks."

He laughed, but Harry's a clean-freak, empties out the ashtray while I'm still smoking. He's trying to get me to quit. I told him I would if he let me suck his dick every time I get a yen for a cigarette. Some day I'll go too far and gross him out.

Mr. Cleary was as good as his word. The hinges on the kitchen cabinets have new screws and the radiators stopped banging and hissing. Then, just a few days after I moved in, I came home and found the place full of furniture—sofa-bed, easy chair, table, lamps, even pots and dishes. At first I thought I had walked into the wrong apartment. I offered him a hundred dollars, but he said he would only take fifty, for his labor. A previous tenant left it all behind and it was just lying in the basement where it wasn't doing anyone any good, he said.

I've never owned a complete set of furniture, I mean everything bought at one time, even if it's second-hand. My husband and I always had hand-me-downs. That's what happens if you get pregnant when you're sixteen. The same people who would feel obligated to give you a thousand dollars if you were marrying with a nice flat stomach in front of a nice rabbi with a nice lawyer or doctor for a bridegroom, when you get hitched the way I did and can really use some cash for diapers and baby clothes, they send over the broken lamp they were planning to throw out anyway or the raggedy sofa they would have given to a thrift shop and then written off their taxes. And they think they've done a big mitzvoth.

Harry seems as pleased with my windfall as I am. I sensed he was a little nervous when I was living in the Tudor Arms and hating every minute of it. Since the furniture arrived we've been spending half our time here and half at his place in Brooklyn. We both work in Manhattan and most of the shows and concerts and restaurants we go to are located here as well. Brooklyn still seems like the end of the world to me. If we ever do decide to live together, it would make sense for us to live at my place. But I'll never suggest that, because Harry loves Brooklyn. He's near Prospect Park and likes to bring his four-year-old there to play ball and collect acorns. He's a cute little guy, the boy, reminds me of Kevin when he was that age. Harry has him on alternate weekends, which means we really can't go anywhere unless we find a babysitter. But I knew right from the start he had a child, I'm not complaining. I just wish he didn't feel so guilty about it. He's very protective, gives in to the boy's every whim.

The radiator started hissing and giving off a bad smell. I left a message for Mr. Cleary on his answering machine. I figured he'd come up to fix it while I was at work, but when I got home from work there he was, holding some sort of rubber hose, one end of which was inside the radiator and the other end sticking out of the window. It gave me a start, finding him there, but he didn't even acknowledge my presence until he had finished with the radiator and replaced the cover on it.

"Shouldn't be a problem now," he said. "I bled it and replaced the air valve. Would you mind," he said, only then looking my way, he might have been talking to himself up to that point, "if I washed my hands?"

I told him to go ahead. I'm used to pulling off my pantyhose as soon as I come through the door each night. Instead, I had to stand and watch while he washed up—he chose the kitchen sink—lathering and turning his hands inside and over each other like a surgeon scrubbing for an operation.

"Can I offer you a cup of coffee?" I asked purely for form's sake, I was supposed to meet Harry for supper in less than an hour.

He said, "Coffee would be lovely," drying his hairy hands with paper towels.

"All I have is de-caf." The only other items in my refrigerator were two containers of blueberry yogurt and half a quart of skimmed milk.

He sat down at the Formica table he had brought up for me from the basement. The kitchen is plenty big enough for one person to move about comfortably, but a couple of strangers in there at the same time is another matter.

"De-caf's fine."

He added milk and a couple spoonfuls of sugar. His hands were pink beneath the mat of black hair covering them, he must have used very hot water to wash them. The hair on his head was thick but almost completely gray.

"I would have come up earlier," he said, "but my wife needed me." He took a sip of coffee, found it too hot and put it down again. I figured I'd give him five minutes to finish his coffee, then go change in the bathroom if he still hadn't left. "She's a paraplegic. Car accident. I feed her, bathe her. Take care of her...necessities."

I saw a frail, gray stalk of a woman with big sunken eyes hunched over in a wheelchair. Not exactly a sex symbol.

"Does she ever get out of the house?"

"I take her out for walks. Push her over to look in the store windows. Watch the kids in the schoolyard. Sometimes I take her to Sunday mass—they made the church wheelchair-accessible last year. Mostly she watches TV. Soap operas, game shows. All the daytime woman's programs. In the evening we play canasta and watch a video. She likes Westerns, Clint Eastwood. When we were younger, before the accident, we took trips out West. She loves open spaces, the mountains."

"No children."

"No," he said. "Some day I'd like to get her out of the city, move out West permanently. The change would do her good."

"She grew up there, in the West?"

He looked up and smiled a wry half-smile that must have been a real attention-getter in his youth. "She was born and raised not two blocks from here."

I saw their life together: perfect devotion on his part, eternal gratitude on his wife's. A kind of eternal vigil to what had been and to all that could not be. Talk about for better or for worse.

"I'm very sorry, Mr. Cleary."

He nodded. "We're lucky, actually, to have each other. Plenty of folks who can walk around just fine can't stand the person they're married to. But we enjoy each other's company. What happened was

God's will and we accept it." Sip, sip and suddenly the coffee was gone. "But you want your apartment back, so I'll be on my way."

"He might not even have a wife. He could just be suckering you in, setting you up. First you go to the basement alone with him, then he gives you an apartmentful of furniture. Now he lets himself in and waits for you to come home from work."

Harry had me thinking, I won't deny it. I admit I'm not a very good judge of character.

"But he's obviously devoted to her," I said.

"And she's a paraplegic. What kind of sex life do you suppose they have? Sure he's 'devoted.' I'm devoted too—to my mother. That doesn't mean she meets my sexual needs."

Part of my problem is I can't imagine anyone is going to make a pass at me unless they're crazy or desperate—or because they make a pass at every woman. Harry tells me men are looking at me all the time on the street, but I find that hard to believe. Or if they are it's because some men look at anything with tits. I'm not ugly and I have a decent shape, but I never dress so as to draw attention to myself. I don't *want* to be noticed, except by Harry, of course.

The next time I ran into Mr. Cleary he was mopping the lobby floor. "Good morning," he said, pausing his mop when he saw how apprehensive I was about walking on the wet. "Radiator okay?"

"Fine," I said, still worried about slipping and falling, I'm very near-sighted. But then I remembered what Harry said, so I added, "Works perfect now. Thanks again."

"My pleasure," he said, resuming his mopping like I was just a tenant like any other. "Mind the wet on your way out."

Monday, January 30

Three days later—that's yesterday—I picked up the *Times* on my way to work. A few minutes later I'm on the train, glancing at the headlines on the front page and metro sections.

"Super Takes Own Life, Wife Survives."

I start to read, having at this point more than a passing interest in superintendents.

'The building superintendent of a co-op on 9th Avenue in Manhattan has died as a result of inhaling gas fumes in what the police are describing as an apparent suicide pact. Edward J. Cleary, Jr. was pronounced dead-on-arrival at St. Vincent's Hospital. His wife, Emma Cleary, is in critical condition.

'There was no suicide note, according to police spokesperson, Angela Rodriguez.

'One of the building's tenants reported smelling gas fumes when she went to the building's basement where the Clearys lived....'

I went on reading but with the sense of unreality I sometimes get in dreams: nice try, but too far-fetched. I only managed not to miss my stop because the train was delayed at the East Broadway station, I barely squeezed through the closing doors in time.

It's the first time I've ever known anyone who's killed himself.

When I reached the methadone center Sarah said I looked like I was coming down with something. I showed her the *Times* article.

"You knew him?"

"He's the super for my building." (Not a co-op, by the way, the papers always manage to get at least one fact wrong.) "A couple days ago he was telling me how happy he and his wife were. She's a paraplegic—was—still is, I guess, she's still alive. He was saying how lucky they were to have each other, how plenty of people who can move around just fine don't enjoy each other's company the way they did. He said he wanted to take her out West because she loved the open spaces and the mountains. He was sitting in my kitchen, drinking a cup of de-caf, I didn't have any real coffee in the house because my gynecologist told me to cut down. And all I was thinking was, how can I get rid of him, I have to meet Harry in half an hour...."

Sarah made me sit down right there in reception between two junkies who were waiting for their daily doses. She told one of them to go get me some water from the cooler, then insisted I drink it. I never touch anything handled by a client without washing my hands afterward, never mind drink from it, but I did as she asked.

"It makes absolutely no sense," I said. "None. Zilch."

"People deceive themselves, honey. Sometimes they say what they want to believe."

She asked if I was okay now. I said I was, she had to get back to the switchboard and the waiting clients.

"I just feel so bad, for them both," I told Harry when he called me back, I never can reach him directly. "The poor man was probably trying to tell me something, but all I could think was, how can I get rid of him so I wasn't late meeting you for dinner."

"What happened is not your fault, Deirdre. You not only didn't throw him out, you sat and listened to him."

"But maybe not enough."

"If he had wanted to tell you something, you gave him ample opportunity. The man was deranged, suicidal."

"I know," I said—Harry always calls me Deirdre when he's losing patience with me, just like my mother—"I just wish I could have said something so that it never happened."

"What more could you do? Let him move in with you?

"That's not what I meant."

"I'm sorry," he said, recovering his professional tone, the one he must use with clients. "I just hate to see you beat up on yourself like this."

"It's just so *sad*. I mean, he was alive, he was saying what a good marriage he had. They were making plans."

Then I lost it, started sobbing like it was someone close to me who died. Harry said I should take the rest of the day off, come meet him for lunch, then go back to his place in Brooklyn.

"What about the police?" I said. "Won't they want to question the building's tenants?"

"You can speak to them on the phone."

He had to go. He has a caseload close to two hundred and they never give him a minute's peace. I told my supervisor I was taking the rest of the day off. Only, instead of heading downtown I took the train back up to Greenwich Village.

VI

The Least I Can Do

The Same Day

St. Vincent's is not my favorite hospital, no hospital is, but I felt it was the least I could do to offer some comfort to Mrs. Cleary. I had to lie my ass off to get into the ICU. I told them I was her first cousin, I figured they might suspect something if I said I was her sister, though most people take me for Irish, even fellow Jews.

She was unconscious, in a coma I supposed, though I didn't ask. She was hooked up to half a dozen medical gizmos--heart monitor, oxygen, IV, plus a few I didn't recognize even with all the TV doctor shows I watch. Her long gray hair lay on the pillow in a disheveled state. Her complexion was pink and healthy. I could see the shape of her body underneath the heavy white sheet. Lying there, she didn't look crippled, and I thought, this was how her husband had seen her each night when they went to bed, pretty much the same as she must have looked before the automobile accident, except maybe for the grayness of her hair. Thinking about what Harry said, I wondered if they managed to make love, if she could physically tolerate it and if she felt anything like a whole woman would.

I came closer and looked down at the plastic identification bracelet on her wrist. The name Cleary was visible, but only the last three letters of her first name were showing—"-lyn." The *Times* said her name was Emma. Her hand lay motionless on top of the sheet, far more still than the hand of someone who was merely sleeping. I put my own hand on it. It felt warm and very much alive.

"I'm very sorry, Mrs. Cleary," I said, not having a clue what I should say under the circumstances, assuming of course there was the slightest chance she could hear me. "I hope you get better. If you do, maybe we could be friends."

I was late for my lunch with Harry, but I didn't tell him why. I felt guilty, not just about not telling him but because I thought he would disapprove of what I had done. I know what that sounds like, but most of the time I stand up for my rights nowadays, not that I have to, Harry is the most understanding man I've ever known.

I actually felt better, more composed, after visiting Mrs. Cleary, so I decided to go back to work after lunch with Harry. He objected, said I was still emotionally distraught even if I didn't realize it. I usually take his advice, I like the way he fusses over me, nobody's done that since I was a child. But Mr. Cleary wasn't, after all, anyone close to me. I told Harry I'd stay over with him in Brooklyn that weekend if he liked, and he perked up.

No sooner did I get back to my office than the telephone rang. It was the police, they must have got my number out of Mr. Cleary's tenant directory. The officer—Donegan or Donnelly—wanted to know how well I had known the deceased.

"Not very. I just moved in a couple weeks ago."

"Did you notice any unusual behavior on his part during that time?" He seemed to be reading the questions off a piece of paper.

"He fixed some things in my apartment. Put up a window gate."

"Did he ever say anything that might indicate he was contemplating suicide?"

I said no, though of course in retrospect virtually everything someone who did what Mr. Cleary did can seem like a warning sign.

"Were you aware that his wife was a paraplegic?"

"I was."

"He told you?"

"Yes."

"Did you ever meet Mrs. Cleary?"

"No," I said. "Not...at least, while her husband was alive."

"Come again?"

"I went to see her," I said, embarrassed, not because of any inference the cop might or might not draw but because of the subterfuge I had used to get into the ICU. "At the hospital."

"When was this?"

"This morning. Right after I read in the newspaper about what happened. I thought it was the least I could do."

"You went to see her at St. Vincent's?"

"Of course, she was still in a coma, so the conversation was pretty one-sided, you could say."

"Ms. Davis, is your home phone number still 555-5823?"

"Yes. I think so. I just had it installed."

He thanked me for my cooperation, but I got a feeling I would be hearing from him again. I probably shouldn't have mentioned that I went to see Mrs. Cleary, but I can't lie. I read somewhere that paranoid people are like that. We're so sure we'll eventually be found out that we try to head off our accusers by confessing to everything right up front.

This is the first time in my life that anything like this has ever come so close to touching me personally. Apart from that business with the police when Tim Davis and I were hauled into court for having sex, I've never had any contact with the law, and certainly not with the kind of tragedy that befell the Clearys. What they did, tried to do, is the kind of stuff that ends up on the front page of the tabloids (the *Post* did, in fact, run the story there, though the mayor's chest pains stole the big banner headline). It's always been something that happens to someone else—"news," not reality. It certainly doesn't happen to someone you've had coffee with, someone who's told you how lucky he was to have the wife he did and how much he was looking forward to a better future with her, and I mean a future right here in this life.

Friday, February 3

I've heard nothing from officer Donegan/Donnelly. But I did go back to see Mrs. Cleary, just this morning in fact. I'd have waited till after work, only I didn't want Harry to know. I don't know why, I just have a feeling he would object and I don't want to get him upset.

This time I didn't have to lie about who I was, though I was ready to, I had spent the time waiting for the subway concocting a set of aunts and uncles to flush out the details of our kinship.

She was out of the ICU, having regained consciousness the previous afternoon. The nurse warned me that my cousin didn't remember anything about how she had ended up in the hospital. She didn't even know her husband was dead. The doctors were still assessing her for brain damage. That's all she needs, I thought, to go along with her useless legs. She might not, the nurse further cautioned me, even remember who I was. I replied with a straight face (I've never cared for anyone in a medical uniform) that I would be discrete.

It was a bit of a shock, my first sight of her lying there, her eyes open and her head turned toward the window on the other side of the room. It was just as if the last time I saw her she had simply taken leave of her body for a while. It had gone on breathing and otherwise functioning without her, but it might have been anybody's body, an empty vessel. But today, she—someone—was very much back inside.

"Hello," I said.

She didn't seem to hear me, or assumed I was talking to her roommate, a very old woman asleep in the other bed. It was only when I stepped further into the room and entered her peripheral vision that her eyes moved, and then her head.

"I'm Deirdre Davis," I said. "A neighbor of yours."

I stepped closer to the bed. Her hands lay outside the sheet just as they had the last time I visited. An IV was still attached to one wrist like a permanent tether.

"You saw my husband?" she said in a quiet but surprisingly melodic voice, a girl's voice, that seem to come from someone other than herself.

"No, I haven't."

"He was hurt," she said, "in the crash."

I nodded. Her eyes were large and so blue they seemed artificially colored like a child's crayon drawing.

"His legs," she said. "The doctors...are you a doctor?"

"No, I'm not."

"... they say he may never walk again."

"I'm very sorry, Mrs. Cleary."

She nodded. I'd seen that nod any number of times--women like Mrs. Cleary talking on the street about their ailing husbands when they run into each other during their trips to the supermarket, women who get their hair dyed and set every Friday like clockwork and haven't missed Sunday mass since the days they were still in their parents arms. That nod always seemed to convey a kind of ghoulish satisfaction that this is how life is, so you might just as well expect the worst and didn't I tell you so. She stared up at me as if waiting for contradiction, just as I have seen those women do, though usually women much older than she, when they're relating to one of their twins how a husband had been "fine one moment and, sure enough, didn't he just keel over dead." But today for the first time I saw it wasn't the macabre that motivated them, this was their version of bravado, their way of coping. And even though Mrs. Cleary had got it wrong, even though she was mixing up what happened two days ago with an accident ten years earlier that had left herself, not her husband, permanently crippled, the stoical faces of all those widows and fatherless daughters seemed to parade before me.

"I was the lucky one, she said with a flirty smile. "God protected me."

I didn't dare try to speak. I had come here to give comfort, I had thought.

A nurse came in with a tray of pills in tiny paper cups.

"Oh, another?" Mrs. Cleary said. But she accepted a glass of water from the young woman and swallowed the pills one right after the other. Only then did she say, "I hate pills, don't you, Doctor?" Meaning me.

I walked down to Sheridan Square to the little park there. An old man was feeding pigeons, they were swarming all round him. I hate pigeons and try to avoid them, I'm afraid of catching something.

My husband used to make fun of me, the way I rushed Kevin away from any. Kids love pigeons, especially when they're toddlers and can barely walk, pigeons are one of the few living things they can intimidate. But I needed to sit somewhere in peace, so I chose a bench as far away from the pigeon-feeder as possible. Feeding them is against the law but you'd never know it.

It's one thing to know that horrible things can happen to people, it's quite another to see it with your own eyes. I kept thinking that could be me lying in that hospital bed, the victim of one of Tim Davis's loony notions. Once, he gave me a copy of Flannery O'Connor's short stories to read. I read about half of them, she's a fantastic writer but she also had a few screws seriously loose, if you ask me. That one about the boy launching himself into the afterlife by committing suicide, all that theological stuff, it's just plane sicko, like those plaster saints who bleed and the body parts they keep in crucifixes for people to kiss when they bring them out every year on certain days. O'Connor gave me the creeps the same way, though I remember I did like one story, "Everything That Rises Must Converge," there wasn't much of that weird Catholic stuff in that one.

A man sat down next to me, business suit, expensive tie and haircut. Actually, he sat down on the other section of the bench, there's a curved iron armrest in between.

"Nice day," he says.

I actually hadn't noticed what kind of day it was. I checked to see and sure enough he was right.

"Rain tonight, though," he added.

"Is that right?"

"Seventy percent chance after midnight. Clearing by morning. Sunny and milder tomorrow."

I couldn't help smiling, he sounded just like a weatherman. He had a wide wedding band on his left hand and he wasn't trying to hide it.

"On your lunch hour?" he said.

I told him I had just been to visit a friend in St. Vincent's.

"Nothing serious, I hope."

"Serious enough."

"I'm sorry to hear that. I wish him well."

I started to get teary, it doesn't take much these days. Naturally, I didn't have a tissue in my bag. He offered me his handkerchief, a really expensive one, I would no more blow my nose in it then I would in the sleeve of his suit jacket. I just dabbed at my eyes the way I'd seen characters do in movies.

"Would you like to go somewhere for a couple coffee?" he said. "Might make you feel better."

I said I'd already had two cups of coffee, but I wouldn't mind a drink. I couldn't believe I said it, only I felt so damn blue, the thought of being alone again stone sober was just too awful to contemplate.

He took me to a nearby bar, I'd been there back before the Village became overrun with yuppies. I had two stingers, then asked him to make love to me.

I've never done anything like this before. It took me ten years to work up the nerve to go to bed with someone else after Tim Davis started cheating on me, and even then it wasn't sex I wanted, then or now, but asking a man to hold you in his arms without having sex is like asking a firecracker not to go off after lighting it. Besides, it's not really true I didn't want him to make love to me. I did. I wanted it because of Emma/Evelyn Cleary, because she couldn't have it and I still could.

I didn't feel anything for this man like what I feel for Harry. When he was on top of me I kept thinking about Emma Cleary and Molly Bloom, only I was saying to myself, "No, no, I won't. No, I won't, no," and I started to giggle, I never drink that early in the day and those stingers had my head reeling. Tony, that was the man's name, asked what was so funny. I said, "Nothing," I figure to he wouldn't get the joke. But I guess I had ruined it for him because he went limp inside me, and even though I assured him my amusement had nothing to do with us, it was just something I had read in a book, he climbed off and started to get dressed. I guess I was lucky he didn't beat me up.

VII

Kevin Comes to Visit

Wednesday, March 1

Kevin called to say he's coming to New York.

I could hardly believe it. I didn't think I'd ever see him again unless I hopped on a plane to Indiana.

"What about your job?"

"I'm taking a week off. I've been there almost eight months, I have the time."

I was still too pleased and amazed to say anything else until he asked, "Will it be okay? I don't want to upset you or anything."

Him upset *me*. He's been on medication for the past two years, has had Joe Stalin for a father and a field mouse for a mother, but he worries about upsetting me. But that's Kevin all over—the sweetness, the diffidence.

I started to cry, and now he was sure he had upset me.

"I'm crying," I said through a soggy tissue, "because I'm just so happy at the prospect of seeing you. I love you so much, Kevin."

"I love you too, mother."

"Where will he sleep?" Harry asked when I told him.

"I'll buy a cot."

"And you'll sleep on the air mattress?"

"Why not? That's where I've been sleeping for the past two months."

He didn't say anything else, but I could tell he didn't like the idea. Harry is pretty conventional about some things. The idea of someone's mother sleeping on the floor violates one of those conventions.

I stocked the refrigerated with Kevin's favorite snacks—those little cups of chocolate putting, the kind that's laced with swirls of caramel; fresh lox and cream cheese to go with the bagels we could buy on Houston Street, we could walk there together; two six packs of Fanta orange soda. His flight was due at Newark airport at six p.m. I wanted to go over to meet him, but he told me to wait at my apartment, he didn't even want me to meet the shuttle bus at the Port Authority terminal.

At three p.m. I started checking with the airline to see if his flight had left on time. By five I had called three times. There was still no anticipated delay, but when the plane didn't arrive I couldn't understand what the problem was until I looked out the window and saw there was a thunderstorm in full swing. My doorbell finally rang at eight, and there he was, a bit damp from his dash from the cab, a grown man with a five o'clock shadow. I didn't even wait for him to come inside to throw my arms around his moist neck.

"I still can't believe you're here," I said as I put on some water to make a cup of tea. He said he had already eaten on the plane, but he always liked a cup of tea, even when he was just a little guy.

"I'm here all right," he said, no sign of nervousness, it was me who was racing around like a nut, kissing him every time I passed his chair. I couldn't get over how grown-up he looked. It seemed the last time I took a good look he was a fuzzy-cheeked teenager, and the time before that he was waddling around in diapers. His body felt hard and thick when I embraced him, and each time I kissed his rough cheek I felt embarrassed, as if I were kissing a stranger who was somehow possessed by the little boy I remembered as my Kevin.

"Later we'll go out and get something to eat."

"Whatever you prefer."

I hadn't eaten anything since lunchtime, but I didn't realize it, I was so filled up by his presence. The last time I saw him he was virtually homeless, a refugee from his father's relentless hectoring and my own sense of powerlessness. No medication could by itself account for his present self-possession, sipping his hot tea, the bag still in, no milk or sugar. He was a man now, just as Harry was, or his own father, or my father. I only kissed him one more time that night, just before he lay down on the cot he insisted on making up for himself in the short end of my L-shaped living room, while I bedded down as usual in the long end not far from the radiator Mr. Cleary had stopped from banging just before he took his life.

As I lay watching the clouds race eastward over Ninth Avenue—it continued to rain off and on all the evening--I felt incredibly lucky. Lucky for escaping from a suffocating and pointless marriage, lucky for having a man like Harry in my life when so many other women lived lonely celibate lives, lucky for having a son like Kevin.

The next morning we were both up early—we're both early risers, it's only Tim Davis who likes to sleep in. I thought I'd take him down to the Village for pancakes, then we could walk around, maybe stop in a couple bookstores. But just as we were on our way out the door the phone rang. It was Sgt. Donnelly from Midtown South. He wanted to know if I could stop by the station house, he had a few questions about the Clearys.

That was enough to take away any appetite I had. At first I didn't say anything to Kevin about what was putting me out of sorts. But he's a smart kid, you can't put something by him.

"The police just want to ask a few questions. They're probably talking to everyone in the building who had any contact with Mr. Cleary in the days before it happened. I'm sorry," I said. "I didn't want anything to spoil our time together."

"How long will it take?"

"A half hour. An hour."

"Do you think you'll feel up to stopping by the library on 42nd Street afterward? There's an exhibit of Dickens manuscripts I'd like to see."

"Of course. We can have lunch in the new outdoor cafe in Bryant Park."

Manhattan South is just as grimy and gray as any other police precinct. I've never much liked cops, not since that time my father had Tim Davis arrested for statutory rape, though Tim has always been a police groupie himself. He can't pass one by without giving a big hello. Once, in Riverside Park, we were having a sort of picnic. Tim had brought a six pack of beer, expensive imported beer, I can't remember which brand. It was a hot day. A couple young patrolmen came by. Tim knew they couldn't accept a beer from someone while they were in uniform, so he opened two bottles and put them on top of the wall that separates the park from the Westside Highway. He whistled softly to get the cops' attention, pointed to the bottles, then returned to our blanket. Sure enough, the patrolmen came back for the beers, giving Tim a little salute as they made off to a secluded nook to enjoy them while some woman got raped.

Sgt. Donnelly is a paunchy, gray man in a sloppy gray suit that should have been given to charity years ago. He sat me down next to his gray desk in the middle of a big room full of other detectives and their own gray desks. He thanked me for cooperating.

I was pretty nervous. Authority always makes me feel both guilty and angry. He asked me how long I had been living on Ninth Avenue, where I had lived previously, when was the last time I saw Edward Cleary—many of the same questions he had already asked me on the phone. I gave the exact same responses. Then he laid the big one on me.

"Did Mr. Cleary ever give you anything, Ms. Davis?"

"Like, a gift?"

"That's what I had in mind."

"Why would he be giving me something, I hardly knew him. He was the super, I was a tenant."

Donnelly looked up from whatever it was he was writing in his notes. He had small watery eyes like my father. I wondered if he was nearsighted as well but too vain to wear glasses.

"What about furniture? According to our information, Mr. Cleary provided you with a sofa, tables, chairs, kitchen set," he said, reading from his notes again. When he looked up this time his little blue eyes seemed to have no trouble fixing on me.

"I had just moved in. I had no furniture, nothing. I was living in a furnished room. He said it was stuff a former tenant left behind. I offered to pay him for it, but he said he would only take fifty dollars, for his labor."

"You paid him fifty dollars?"

"Yes."

"In cash?"

"Yes."

He visibly relaxed and looked at me this time as if he were confronting someone entirely different from the woman who had sat down opposite his desk a few minutes ago.

"Were you aware, Ms. Davis, that the furniture he provided you with was his wife's?"

"Of course not."

"Furniture they bought before her accident. Mrs. Cleary is a paraplegic. She was in an automobile accident a number of years back."

He questioned me about my "relationship" with the Clearys. Then he asked about my own marriage, and I imagined he saw all sorts of possibilities in the fact that I had separated from my husband shortly before moving into Edward Cleary's building and accepting the gift of his wife's furniture. Nevertheless, I think I put on a pretty good face. It's one thing for me to be afraid of cops, it's another to feel that someone is accusing me unjustly. He finally realized he had gotten all he was likely to get out of me and said I could go.

I tried not to let it show, how rattled I was, but Kevin picks up on that sort of thing.

"We don't have to go to the library if you're not feeling up to it."

"Don't be silly," I said. "If I could put up with your father for twenty-five years, I can take some questioning by a fat-assed flat-foot."

I knew by the look on his face, as if I had just stuck out my foot and deliberately tripped him, that I had said the wrong thing.

"I'm sorry, Kev."

"That's okay."

"No, I mean it. I should know better. Sometimes I think I'm just a big kid myself, that's why it was so easy for someone like Tim Davis to boss me around. That's why I couldn't protect you better than I did. I'm sorry about that too," I said, taking his arm and going up on tiptoe to kiss him. He turned bright red, I guess some of the people on Fifth Avenue must have noticed. "I love you so much. You have no idea."

The steps of the library were covered with office workers on their lunch hour, you had to step around them, and where there weren't people, there were pigeons waiting for handouts. You wouldn't catch *me* eating anything there.

Inside the library it was cool and quiet. I used to bring Kevin with me when I was writing my masters thesis and had some advanced research to do. We brought along a children's book or borrowed one from the lending library in the building's basement. He sat contentedly while I tracked down whatever tome I needed, then took notes for an hour or two. No fuss, no whining for an ice cream or to go to the bathroom every ten minutes. When he did have to go I accompanied him up to the third-floor men's room, but then he was on his own. He could have been molested in there, but I never gave it a second thought.

The Dickens exhibit was right there in the lobby, all the big exhibits usually are. Tim Davis used to drag me down to see a collection of rare medieval manuscripts or the papers of Anthony Trollope or Jonathan Swift, two of his favorite authors back when he still bothered to read something other than Roman Catholic theology. Afterward we lunched on the grass behind the library, back when the park was still a drug haven, Jamaican pot dealers moving freely among the suits and mini-dresses from nearby office towers. Sometimes Tim even made a buy.

After half an hour Kevin and I had both had our fill of the exhibit—his father would pore over them until my back ached—and we headed back down Fifth Avenue. Kevin had hardly spoken, but he looked content with our outing thus far. Tim Davis would have been jabbering about what had been left out of the exhibit, the politics that mandated which scholars had been authorized to mount it, etc. He was, is, a brilliant man, I don't deny it. The fact that he never got any further than assistant professor at a mediocre Catholic girls college is no indication of his potential, any more than is his current obsession with religion. It takes more than brains to be a success in this life, something I've only recently come to realize, hopefully not too late.

We had lunch at McDonald's—Kevin's choice, I never go into one of those places. He ate two Big Macs, I nibbled at a fish fillet. It might have been fifteen years earlier. Back then he always insisted we eat lunch at McDonald's or Burger King, it was the one bribe he required to sit quietly while I did my work in the library. One Big Mac was enough to satisfy him then, but he always had fries and a thick shake as well. Today he merely drank a Coke.

As I watched him eat I kept seeing the child I had loved so desperately and neglected so shamelessly. I was little more than a child myself then, a rather bitter child, having had to go from mid-adolescence straight into motherhood, when other girls were still thinking about what they would wear to the next dance or making plans for college. Instead, I was changing diapers and staying up half the night studying to get the high school diploma that had been denied me by my pregnancy. I couldn't help blaming Kevin for my predicament, as if he were somehow waiting in the wings for one of those cheap condoms to break. That's all it took, one time. It was stupid, blaming Kevin who was actually a victim of his parents' youth and ineptitude, but you can't help what you feel and I had felt trapped and betrayed by my own all-too-fecund flesh.

"Is there someplace else you'd like to go, a museum? There's a Van Gogh exhibit at the Whitney."

"Actually, if it's okay with you I'd like to lie down for a while. The medication makes me sleepy this time of day."

This was the first time he had mentioned his medication. I had seen him place two prescription bottles on the kitchen countertop the morning after he arrived, but I deliberately avoided saying anything. I knew he was on an anti-psychotic, but I didn't want to embarrass him.

"Should we take the bus, are you too tired to walk?"

"Actually, I'd prefer to walk. It's one of the amenities I miss most about New York. In Indiana nobody walks."

When we got back to the apartment he lay down on the cot and I flopped down on the air mattress with one of my mysteries, mysteries being all I'm able to focus my attention on these days. After ten minutes I assumed he had dozed off, but then I heard, "I never realized how small his readership was. The notes said it was just a few thousand for some of his novels."

It took me a moment to realize he was talking about Dickens. But then I recalled how when he was younger he would suddenly comment on something that had happened days, even weeks, earlier as if he had been thinking about virtually nothing else in the interim. His comments usually came after he had just been put into bed for the night, when I was about to turn out the light or was checking to see if his backpack was in order for the next school day. "Georgia didn't want slavery," he'd say, already tucked into his cot, a more substantial version of the one he was napping on today. "That's what Mr. Arney said."

"Is that right?" I'd reply, my own thoughts on the chores I had to do before I could call it a day myself. At first, his delayed observations seemed just a child's ploy to gain a few extra minutes of wake time. But they were actually the way his mind works, always worked, mulling things over as if *in camera*, only to present some new conclusion long after the slow process of rumination is complete.

"Maybe they felt sorry for the slaves," he said, "because the convicts in Georgia were brought to American against their will like the slaves were."

"Maybe," I said.

"But then they gave in, like the rest of the colonies."

"Don't forget your lunch in the morning."

"Slavery was a terrible thing, wasn't it, Mom."

"It certainly was. Good night."

"Mr. Arney said it was as bad as the Holocaust."

"Mr. Arney is entitled to his opinion."

"He said more slaves died during the trip from Africa."

"Good night."

"Mom?"

"What is it, Kevin? I have things to do."

"I'm glad I'm not black."

As I lay that afternoon fifteen years later, remembering, I felt so bad for the way I had neglected him that I started to cry. I cry at the drop of a hat these days, I was never like this before. I tried to stifle it, but Kevin must have heard because he asked if I was okay.

"Yes," I said. "I just couldn't help thinking, you know, about the past and everything."

"Don't feel bad, Mom. You did the best you could."

"Which isn't saying much."

"Hey, I didn't turn out so bad, did I?"

"You certainly didn't."

"So, there you go."

VIII

Two Old Ladies and Some Chocolates

Tuesday, March 4

I saw Kevin off this morning. When his cab pulled away I felt like a chunk of my heart had just gone with him. People say something like that all the time, I know, but I actually felt a pain in my chest. He called when he reached the airport, and again when he touched down in Indiana. I tried to keep the tears out of my voice, he assured me he'd be back in six months.

After I hung up, all I could think was, what now? I had spent the first twenty-five years of his life resenting him. I saw to it he was fed, had clean clothes and whatever love I could manage. But I hardly ever missed him, not even when he moved away a couple years ago to join a therapeutic community. But this morning I felt the way I imagine a suicide must feel when the last reason for going on living has been taken from them, a kind of panic I can only remember feeling in nightmares. It passed after I was able to reach Harry, but I didn't dare tell him how bad I felt. I never understood what people were talking about when they said how awful they felt when a child left home. To me a child's leaving should seem like a long-overdue reprieve.

I decided I would go to visit Mrs. Cleary. But when I presented myself at St. Vincent's reception, the woman told me the patient had been discharged. I couldn't imagine their sending her home, crippled as she was, but the receptionist wouldn't give me any further information until I said I was a close family member and demanded to know where my half-sister had been taken. I don't know what got into me. I almost never cause a scene, certainly not on my own behalf, only when Kevin or his father's been involved. Finally some kind of administrator was summoned and asked me for identification. She then told me Mrs. Cleary had been transferred to a nursing home on the Lower East Side. She wrote the address in my appointment book. It was way over in the East Village, I didn't even know they had nursing homes in that part of town.

Hospitals are bad, but nursing homes are the pits, I pray to God I never end up in one. The one where they sent Emma Cleary could serve as a horror-movie set—bare gray walls, muscle-bound orderlies, tightly coifed nurses who look like they get their recreation torturing newborn kittens. And not a doctor in sight.

The receptionist regarded me as if the only visitors they got were accident lawyers and crooked health inspectors. When I told her why I was there she not only relaxed, she lost interest. I had to remind her two more times what my business was before she could be bothered to check to see if a patient by the name of Emma Cleary resided there. When she found no one by that name she actually cheered up.

"Try *Evelyn* Cleary," I said.

"Well, which is it?" she demanded from beneath a frosted dye-job. She reminded me of my Aunt Bella, the doctor's wife, only Bella has it all over this dame for class, even with her twitch.

She finally admitted that such a person as Evelyn Cleary inhabited this house of horrors but then informed me the patient wasn't available to receive visitors because she was having her morning bath.

"I'll wait," I said.

"Suit yourself."

Half an hour later she jerked her thumb toward the long corridor behind the reception desk.

"Any particular room?"

"Two-oh-one. Elevator at the end of the hall."

Mrs. Cleary's bed was cranked to a semi-upright position. The linen looked freshly changed. Her roommate, a very old black woman, was asleep.

"Good morning," I said.

She looked up warily, at least she was alert. Her long gray hair was tied back in a ponytail, but it didn't look especially clean. Her complexion was pink.

"I'm Deirdre Davis. I came to see you in St. Vincent's. We're neighbors."

She still didn't say anything, just watched me take a couple cautious steps toward her bedside.

"How are you feeling?"

She tilted her head to one side and drew down the corners of her mouth.

"You look well. May I?" I said, eyeing an iron chair that looked as if it hadn't been used, much less painted, in the last hundred years.

I didn't know how much of this one-sided conversation I could take, I get very nervous when someone doesn't respond, and the place itself was giving me the creeps.

"I can't tell you how glad I am to see you looking so well," I said, latching on to the one positive thing I could think of.

"Who *are* you?" she said finally.

"A neighbor. The people at St. Vincent's told me you were here. I hope you don't mind. I won't stay long."

"You visited me in the hospital."

"That's right."

"I thought you were a doctor."

"You did. You might have still been a little...disoriented."

"What did you say your name was?"

"Deirdre Davis."

"3F."

"That's right. I moved in just a couple months ago."

"My husband mentioned you."

"Did he?" I had to be careful, I had no idea what they had or hadn't told her.

"Eddie said you weren't especially good-looking. But you're actually very pretty."

"Thank you," I said. "You're a very good-looking woman yourself, Mrs. Cleary."

She smiled the way a woman who has lost most of her beauty does when someone pretends she hasn't.

"Are they treating you well, Mrs. Cleary? Do you have everything you need?"

Her Crayola Crayon-blue eyes regarded me gently, willing to make whatever allowances a fallen human nature required. This was her normal way of looking at the world, I realized, and I understood why her husband loved her.

"It's not exactly the Waldorf," she said. "I had no choice, of course. They couldn't keep me in St. Vincent's indefinitely. I have no money. So," she said, glancing at the piss-colored walls, "here I am."

She might find herself in the ante-room of hell, I thought, but her good humor would prevail. If I had been through what she had, I would be terrified and furious.

"It's very kind of you, Deirdre, to come and see an old lady."

"I believe we're pretty close to the same age, Mrs. Cleary, so you'd better watch who you're calling an old lady."

"You don't look a day over twenty-five."

"I'll be forty in a couple weeks."

She stretched out her hand in a gesture she must have used thousands of times, especially since the automobile accident that confined her movements in so many other ways. I put my own out to meet it. Her long fingers closed on mine like a favorite aunt's.

"Call me Emma," she said.

The next time I visited, the next afternoon, I brought a box of chocolates, two boxes actually, one for her roommate. But the second bed was unoccupied and neatly made up. I didn't ask why.

"They wanted to confiscate them at reception," I said as we dug in like two naughty schoolgirls, I can eat half a box at one sitting. "They said chocolate would be bad for you."

"What they wanted was to get their hands on it for themselves."

"I told them I'd only let you have one."

"My husband bought me chocolates," she said. "For my birthday and our anniversary. Sometimes he brought me something else as well, but he never failed with the chocolates. Never touched them himself. Said they'd rot his teeth."

"I was lucky if my husband remembered to send me a card. Even then, it was always one of those comical ones, never the 'To My Darling Wife' kind. I always wanted to get one of those syrupy cards, just once."

"How long have you been married, Deirdre?" she said, licking her fingertips.

"It would be twenty-five years this September."

"'Would be'?"

"We're separated."

"I'm sorry."

"I should have gotten out of the marriage ten years ago. I just didn't have the guts."

She had stopped eating, but I didn't notice right away, I was trying to find one of those cream-filled jobs. When I looked at her again, her cheerful expression had turned to a frown. She looked her age just then. I thought, I have to remember not to frown too much.

"Really," I said, "it was the best thing I've ever done for myself—maybe the *only* thing."

"Twenty-five years is a long time. Are there children?"

"One. Grown up. Lives in Indiana. Schizophrenic, but he's doing okay. He just came to visit me for a few days."

"Then, we're both widows in a manner of speaking."

She had spoken so matter-of-factly, I wondered if she realized what she had said. The cheerfulness had gone out of her expression, replaced by a look of hardset determination. Her complexion was as flawless as ever, but there were crow's feet next to her eyes and hard indentations at each side of her nose.

"I suspected right away," she said. "As soon as I woke up. But they didn't say anything till I asked."

"You seem...remarkably well-adjusted, if you don't mind my saying so."

"It was God's will. I was lucky to have him for all the years I did."

I had seen people look on the bright side of things before, gritty people who just refused to let bad things, even fate itself, get the best of them. But Emma Cleary was one for the books. Either that or she was in la-la land.

"But tell me more about yourself, Deirdre."

I said there wasn't much to tell. I've never been much for talking about myself, whatever my reasons may be for writing all this down. But talking to Emma Cleary was not the same as talking to other people, not even to Lou-Ann.

As I related how I had fallen in love with Tim Davis and then got pregnant in my senior year of high school, I kept wondering if this was the kind of cathartic feeling Catholics got when they went to confession. I once told Tim Davis I wanted to go to confession just to see what it was like. He said it was impossible, that I would first have to get baptized, become a Roman Catholic. I didn't mind the idea of becoming a Christian, I always thought of myself as a kind of Christian anyhow without ever denying I was Jewish, but after seeing what Catholicism did to my husband I wanted no part of that particular religion.

"You had a rough time," she said. "But at least you have your boy."

I felt a little ashamed when she said that, after all the years I looked on Kevin as just a responsibility. "I'm very grateful for him. I wasn't always, but I realize now how lucky I am. Some people never realize just how much they have, they always insist on seeing the glass as half empty."

"I always said to Eddie, think how much worse it could be. We have each other. We have a halfway decent life."

Her bottom lip began to tremble. She fought back the tears until she felt the touch of my hand on her own.

IX

I Find Out I'm an Onanist

Tuesday, March 21

Harry caught me masturbating this morning. I thought he was still asleep, then he reaches over and grabs my hand in the act. I almost always masturbate in the morning. It relaxes me, prepares me for what I have to deal with that day. Even back when I was a little girl, when I had to face that walk to school, the traffic on the Grand Concourse, the terrors of whether I had really finished all my homework and safely stowed it in my book bag even though I checked it three times before I went to bed and again at least twice before I left the house. The fact that I jerk off doesn't have anything to do with my feelings for him, whether he sexually satisfies me.

But he couldn't understand why I would lie there "stimulating" myself, as he put it, when I could be making love with him, we frequently do in the morning. I told him I was worried about Kevin. I actually had been thinking about how rotten I treated my son when he was a kid, and masturbating helped me not to feel so bad about it.

"You masturbate while you think about your child?" he said. He's a little jealous of Kevin, so I was doubly dumb to mention him.

"Not 'thinking' about him. Trying *not* to think. This is the worst part of the day for me, Harry. I lie here worrying about everything I have to do and thinking about all the ways I've fucked up my life, and other peoples' besides."

"Like Tim Davis?"

"Sometimes," I said, deciding honesty was the best policy--another mistake.

"So you think about your ex-husband and jerk off, but I'm not supposed to get upset by that. You're really just trying to 'relax.'"

"That's right. That's what I'm doing."

I put my arms around him and tried to get at his ear, but of course that was another mistake, he pushed me away.

"I'm sorry, Harry. It's a stupid habit. I don't know why I do it."

"*I* know," he said, pretending not to be so pissed, he is after all a social worker. "It's called onanism. The only person you can ever have good sex with is yourself."

I was really hurt when he said that. Even if it was true, and it's not, he didn't have to say it like that, to my face. What I do is not something I'm proud of, it's just the way I am. Besides, he doesn't have any complaints about the sex we have. He gets it morning, noon and night and six ways to Sunday. He's told me dozens of times he never had such good sex before. He even said he felt like he was a virgin before he went to bed with me.

We made up, sort of, before we took our separate trains to work. I insisted he give me a kiss, he didn't want to, he's very stubborn sometimes. But I knew I could never make it through the day if he didn't give that much of a sign he'd forgiven me. I would be lost without Harry, cast adrift, up the creek without a paddle, pick your cliché. I think I'd rather die, I really do. I used to feel the same way about Tim Davis, even after he started cheating on me. I couldn't stand to go on living with him, I felt so humiliated, but the thought of living without him made me tremble, actually physically shake. That's how I felt this morning when I saw how angry Harry was and that there was the possibility, however slight, that he was would walk out on me.

I took an early lunch hour, told my boss I had a doctor's appointment, then hightailed it up to the East Village to see Emma Cleary.

I spend a lot of time thinking about Emma, a lot more than I do thinking about sex, whatever Harry may believe. It's easy to forget, when she and I are chatting away about the latest political scandal or recounting our respective biographies, that she's in a nursing home not just because she's a cripple but because she and her husband tried to take their lives. Every now and then I remember this when she's talking about her childhood or the earlier days of her marriage, before the accident. I want to ask her about the suicide pact, if that's what it was, but I don't know how to begin or even if I really want to know. A part of me would like to pretend Edward Cleary died of a heart attack and that his wife ended up in this ratty nursing home simply because there was no one to take her in.

I think how I would feel if I were in her shoes, so to speak, if I had been physically crippled and Tim Davis had suggested we end it together. I can't imagine Tim ever wanting to give up his skirts or his circle of intellectual holy-rollers. But then I remember how charismatic that fellow Jim Jones was, the one who poisoned all those people who belonged to his "church," even black people and Jews. Or the kooks who tried to join their brethren waiting behind the comet, kind of like that little boy in Flannery O'Connor's story. Some of those people had PhDs. Wasn't St. Paul a bit of a whacko himself, preaching all that mumbo-jumbo about the end of the world? It isn't inconceivable Tim Davis could have gotten hooked up with one of the more radical cults, as long as he got to help run it. And who knows what sort of nutty idea he might have tried to foist off on me or if I wouldn't have believed him, as long as he didn't try to shove it down my throat the way he usually did. There was probably a time when I would have jumped off the Empire State Building with him, and back when we were teenagers and the whole world seemed dead set against us, who's to say I wouldn't have done something else just as crazy. The papers run two or three stories every year about local Romeos and Juliets who kill themselves because their families won't accept who they've fallen in love with.

But of course Emma and her husband were very much adults when they decided to commit suicide—assuming that was actually what happened, I have only the *New York Times* and Manhattan South as evidence for that particular theory. Maybe what actually happened was that Ed Cleary took it on himself to do away with Emma and himself without first getting his wife's consent. Maybe he just flipped out one afternoon, though there was that bit about giving me their old furniture. It's inconceivable to me she could have thought up the idea on her own. I can't remember the newspapers mentioning any suicide note, and Detective Donnelly never volunteered any information about one. Anyway, if it was an attempted suicide, why aren't they keeping a closer eye on her? I have yet to hear about any psychiatrist coming to visit her, never mind a suicide watch being placed on her bed. Or do they assume that, being a cripple, she isn't capable of taking her life without someone else's help?

All of this is what I think about when I'm talking to her, but what I actually discuss is my job or Kevin or sometimes my relationship with Harry, only of course not anything intimate. I hate it when women do that, talk about their boyfriends or husbands to other women. Some things should remain private. Today Emma noticed I was upset and I told her it was because Harry and I had had a misunderstanding, that was the word I used. I had no intention of telling her or anyone else about my "onanism," so I said that sometimes he felt I didn't pay him enough attention.

She nodded. "Men are like that," she said. "They want you to be thinking about them twenty-four hours a day. When we were first married and before the accident Eddie used to be wildly jealous of every man I talked to. He didn't even want to let me do the food shopping by myself. He said I might strain myself lifting something, but I had a pushcart and I didn't even have to pack the groceries into it, the man in the supermarket did that for me. I like to talk, you can see that for yourself, and I talked to both sexes. And that's what drove Eddie crazy, the way I talked to men so easily. He accused me of flirting. Of course, after the accident he had me all to himself, you could say, and he rarely showed any jealousy anymore, even when we went out for a walk with me in the wheelchair."

I wanted to say something then about Tim Davis, about how he didn't seem to care whether I even existed most of the time, until I left him of course. He seemed to get all the attention he needed from his students and the other women he slept with. I was there just to beat up on, someone to absorb the blows of his kinky psychology, though I guess that's a kind of need as well. But I was tired of thinking about Tim Davis. He preoccupied me so completely when I was living with him, I didn't want him to continue to do so now that he was out of my life.

"Are you planning to get a divorce? "Maybe it's none of my business," she said when I didn't answer right away. "I generally don't believe in divorce myself. Catholics don't, you know."

"Oh, I have no problem with divorce," I said. "I guess I just haven't thought that far ahead."

She smiled the way a teacher I once had used to smile when you gave the wrong answer. That smile made you feel a lot stupider than any reprimand.

"I suppose I should think about seeing a lawyer. To tell you the truth," I said, "I'd just as soon it would all go away. I still live in mortal fear of his turning up at my job again, or even at my apartment, though I've been careful not to give out my address to anyone, not even my employer."

"You could get an order of protection. That way if he comes near you he would be liable to arrest."

"I hadn't thought of that," I said. To tell the truth, the idea of bringing my husband before the legal system, whether it was to get an order of protection or even a divorce, scared the bejesus out of me. All I could think was that he would get his own back for it somehow.

"I'd just as soon leave sleeping dogs lie, as they say."

"You said he's already harassed you once, the time he showed up at your office. I'm not trying to alarm you, Deirdre, but who's to say he won't do so again?"

All of a sudden I felt nauseous. In my fantasy Tim Davis was supposed to disappear into the mists of memory.

"He would never let me divorce him," I said. "Not because he loves me, though maybe he does in some sick way, but because in his mind I belong to him, I'm his property. He's a Catholic himself, you know, a half-assed one, but he's a big fan of St. Paul and he used to hang out with Jesuit priests."

"All the more reason why you'll have to take the initiative yourself. As I said, I personally don't believe in divorce, not for myself, but I don't believe a woman should suffer abuse just because she's legally married to someone, and you seem scared shitless of this man, if you don't mind my saying so."

That was all I needed to hear, of course, just that bit of sympathy in her voice, for the waterworks to start. A nurse happened by just then with Emma's medication and she didn't like what she saw.

"I hope your visitor is not upsetting you, Emma," she said, as if she cared, she was probably only thinking about a law suit. But Emma turned her beatific smile on the woman, reached out to take my hand in her own and said, "This isn't just a visitor, nurse. This is my dearest friend."

X

Tears and Laughter

Friday, March 24

I know now that what I really fear is that I will never really be separated from Tim Davis, that he will manage to remain attached to me like a limb or a tumor. It doesn't matter that I never expect to see or hear from him again, that I feel wedded to Harry and only to him. A part of me remains in that apartment on 121st Street, prisoner to a man I no longer love. I don't need a divorce lawyer, I need a surgeon.

I also hate the idea of getting involved with the legal system after what I went through when I was a teenager. I refuse to serve on juries because I have no faith that any justice ever gets done in the courts, not even for the worst murderers and rapists. But Emma has inadvertently convinced me the only way to end my bondage to Tim Davis is to make a clean break of it, to undo what we had done in City Hall when I was four months pregnant twenty-five years ago.

During my weekly telephone call to my mother in Florida I told her what I'm planning to do. Despite the scurrilous letter Tim Davis sent her, I fully expected her to take his side. They were buddies for most of our married life. She and he discussed the latest books, art, politics, all the things she liked to talk about with her friends in the

Russian Tea Room. She knows our marriage has been a tempestuous one, but once she and Daddy removed themselves a thousand miles away, my domestic problems rarely touched her in any personal way. A couple times I took a plane down to Miami to cry on her shoulder and found a cold stone instead of comforting flesh. My marriage was my own affair, as far as she was concerned, just as it had been up to me to take responsibility for the way I had behaved that resulted in my having to get married in the first place. She didn't have a child of her own until she was well into her thirties, and I've always suspected her of thinking me a careless little fool for not ensuring I didn't get pregnant the way I did.

"End it," she said after I barely began to describe what I was thinking of doing. "End it" would become her mantra for the rest of our conversation, to be invoked every thirty seconds more to shut me up, to end the conversation, than to offer any considered advice. Stupid me, I went on jabbering away about my twenty-some years of marriage, how I thought I had taken reasonable precautions against getting pregnant, how hopeful I had been Tim and I would succeed despite that terrible beginning, slipping in now and then a veiled complaint about how little counseling I received on the subject of sex in my early teens and how abandoned I felt generally throughout the whole ordeal. I could sense her squirming on the other end of the line, but I genuinely wanted her help, however skeptical I was that I would receive any. Besides, I was only giving her a bit of her own back. She's a past mistress of talking out of both sides of her mouth, assuring me she cares but will you look at the time I must run to my fundraiser/book club meeting/tenants group.

Not that I don't have other things to worry about. Harry began acting strange after what happened Wednesday morning. Only, instead of pushing me away he's been coming on to me like gangbusters. Last night he asked would I mind if he watched while I was "doing it." I could feel he was excited just at the prospect of my saying yes, and I thought what the hell, if it makes him happy. But halfway through he decided I should put his organ into my mouth, and then he tried to fellate me at the same time, until we had so many body parts stuffed into each other's orifices that I started to laugh.

"What's so funny?" he said.

His face was so red and his mouth and cheeks so covered with my juices that I laughed even harder. I had no idea at that point how angry he was, I thought he would see how funny the situation was and would laugh along with me. But the next thing I know he's climbing out of bed and pulling on his pants.

"Come back," I said. "I was only laughing at what the two of us must look like."

"Hilarious," he said, his organ still too hard to successfully get his pants closed. That struck me as funny too, and this time he lost his temper entirely and started to call me names, nasty names I never imagined could come out of his mouth, names even Tim Davis never called me.

I was too shocked to reply, shocked and scared because he looked crazy and I was suddenly afraid of him, and Harry is someone I never dreamed I could be afraid of. Some of the milder things he said were that I should only have sex with myself because that was the only kind of real sex I was capable of, and that he understood now why my husband went around with other women if this was what he had to put up with. That last remark made me regret I'd ever confided in him, and made me angry with him for seeming so considerate and understanding that I felt it was safe to open up and make myself vulnerable to a scene such as this.

It wasn't until he had stormed out of the apartment, his shirt still hanging out of his pants, that I realized it was his bed I was lying in and his own home that he had just walked out of. That meant he would be back, probably sooner rather than later, so I quickly got dressed, gathered together the dresses I kept in his closets and stuffed them into a shopping bag. I didn't even bother to put on makeup.

I was afraid he would be waiting for me out on the street and would start another scene, especially after he saw I had removed my clothing from his apartment. But the street, a quiet residential block in Park Slope, was empty. I walked as fast as I could toward the subway, not the one he and I usually take but the "D" train that runs up Flatbush Avenue. I was just as likely to run into him by walking in that direction as in the other, but I wasn't thinking logically, all I wanted was to get out of the neighborhood as fast as I could.

I hadn't felt this kind of fear since the morning I left my husband. I didn't even realize how upset I was until a woman asked if there was anything she could do. I had no idea what she was talking about, I thought she was panhandling or was some kind of religious type. Then I realized the reason she looked so blurry wasn't because I had forgot to clean my glasses but because I was crying. I pulled myself together and slowed down my pace. I was still scared, not at the idea of running into Harry who, despite the things he said would almost certainly never lay a hand on me, but at the prospect of losing him. I had come to think of him as a permanent part of my life even though I knew love affairs usually don't last forever and that I couldn't expect this one to be the exception. But from the first day I met him—he had sent me a referral and decided he would stop by with the client himself, since our offices were not that far from each other—I had felt safe and loved. It was a bizarre reaction, because we scarcely talked about anything but business that day, but I immediately knew I wanted to spend the rest of my life with this man. He later said he had felt the same way, or at least that something strange was going on, but maybe what he really meant was that it was me that was strange and all he really felt was that I looked like an easy lay.

Thinking these kinds of thoughts didn't make it easy to remain dry-eyed, but I managed to make it back to Manhattan without making a spectacle of myself. I was afraid to go back to my apartment, that's the first place he would go looking for me, so I headed over to the East Village to visit Emma Cleary. Of course, Emma saw right away that something was up. I didn't want to go into the gruesome details, I told her Harry and I had had a quarrel.

"Serious?"

"Pretty serious," I said. "He said some things it won't be easy to forget."

Her usually cheerful face became grave in a way I remembered my teachers' becoming back in elementary school when someone in the class did something especially bad like punch another child or curse. It was a look that used to make my bowels come loose even though I was never its object.

"It's partly my fault," I said. "I should have taken the situation more seriously. I guess I hurt his pride."

She didn't say anything. What could she say, I was being so deliberately vague. She was still regarding me with a severe expression, her brow knit tightly, her lips pursed. I knew she had no children of her own and that we were almost the same age, but I felt as if my mother were looking at me. Not my real mother, who would have told me these things happen dear and changed the subject, but the mother I should have had. I wasn't used to this kind of attention. I was much more comfortable being ignored, not just by my mother but by Tim Davis and everyone else.

Finally I couldn't take it anymore, something inside me gave up or gave in, and I started to cry again, only this time it was the full waterworks. Emma held her arms out to me, but I couldn't very well lie down next to her to let her hold me, so we compromised: I sat down beside her and she stroked my hand and rubbed my shoulder. I expected one of the attendants to come in and throw a fit and tell me I couldn't come back to see her anymore, but nothing like that happened. I just sat and cried, and Emma lay there and rubbed, and eventually I dried my eyes and sat back down on the chair again.

"I haven't bawled like that since I was a kid," I said. "I must be cracking up."

"Not at all," she said. "The older I get the more inclined I am to believe the only appropriate response to this world is laughter and tears. Everything else is useless."

It took me a few moments to take in what she had said. Then it struck me that she had just put into words something I had long believed myself without ever quite thinking about it. I started to cry again, then began laughing instead, then crying, until I was alternately crying and laughing, for and at myself, and Emma was doing the same thing, only she was more laughing than crying. This time an attendant, a young black man, did stop to see what was going on. When he saw the two of us laughing like two schoolgirls, the tears streaming down out cheeks, he stood staring in amazement for a few seconds, then just walked away.

XI

I Ride the Broadway Local Again

Tuesday, March 28

Tim Davis is in the hospital. Kevin called me at work, an "opportunistic infection," he said. He's being treated with antibiotics but hasn't responded so far. Needless to say, Kev is in a funk, and I'm not doing so well myself. Kevin didn't say so, but I know he thinks I should pay his father a visit. I keep telling myself there's not much a man can do to me from a hospital bed, especially if he's as sick as Kevin says he is. But telling myself this and believing it are two different things. I never expected to lay eyes on my husband again, at least not willingly, and certainly not under these circumstances. He's always been the healthy one, while I seemed to come down with every virus that was making the rounds. He used to make me tea and toast, boil a chicken for soup, even feed me with a spoon the way Sarah our maid used to do when I was a kid. And then jump into bed beside me, but how can you say no to a man who's lavished such kindness on you? Especially since I usually wasn't as sick as I thought. I would even start thinking that life with him wasn't so bad really, how many men would make chicken soup for you and feed it to you on a spoon? But of course as soon as I was healthy again he would revert to his overbearing ways. Or after a couple days of TLC leave me with my tea and toast to slip out for a bit of fun with some Columbia grad student.

Do I owe it to him to visit him now when he himself is sick, really sick? Does he even want to see me? Kevin is no judge of this because he isn't thinking any more clearly than I am. However badly the man has treated him, Tim Davis is still his father, the man who used to take him camping and to Yankee games, not just the monster who refused him dinner until he had memorized one of St. Paul's epistles. Even so, the boy is just starting to get his own life together and doesn't need this kind of agitation.

"Why not wait a day or two, see how it goes," I told him. "You spoke to him today?"

"This morning."

"And?"

"He sounded weak but not, you know... I'd just feel better if one of us paid him a visit. Just looked in to see how he really is."

I tried to assure him the antibiotics would start kicking in any time now and that his father would be his normal self again in no time. But I only half-believed it. I was thinking about that fellow who created the Muppets who died of some sort of freak infection when he was not much more than fifty. People die by the tens of thousands every year from infections they pick up in hospitals, never mind the ones they come down with on their own.

"I'll call St. Luke's at lunchtime," I told him—I still had a meeting to attend, though by now I felt like I had already put in a full day. Then I verified Kevin's current work number. "We'll take it from there. Okay?"

He said okay, but he sounded like he was in danger of going into one of his depressions, so I told him maybe he should check in with his therapist just to be on the safe side. He said he already had.

"And?"

"She said I should do what I feel. I should do whatever would make it easiest to live with myself, no matter what happens."

"Which is?"

There was silence for a moment. I prayed he wasn't going to cry because my meeting was scheduled to start in less than ten minutes and it was in another building.

"I don't know."

"I'll try to talk to someone at the hospital on my lunch break. Then we'll reevaluate the situation."

I said goodbye and a part of me felt the same way I used to feel when I had finished dressing him for school and pushed him out the door even though I knew he would have to run a gauntlet through a bunch of black kids in the schoolyard. Tim Davis and I thought we were doing something liberal when we chose to send him to the local public school in Harlem instead of to one of the yuppie public schools on the Upper West Side where the other middle-class liberals sent their kids. But it was really Kev who did something socially responsible, not we who went off to our jobs downtown while he suffered at the hands of those black kids who saw him as no less privileged or white just because he sat in the same classroom with them, and they treated him badly as only children can do. I won't go into detail, it's too painful to think about.

Today's wasn't, of course, the same situation, I told myself as I scurried over to my training session on Foley Square. But throughout the rest of the morning while I sat taking notes and then gave my little presentation I felt like I was cheating my son, trying to advance my career while he sat in Indiana worrying about his father.

On the other hand, he knew what he was doing when he said he would feel better if "one of us" went to see Tim Davis. Kevin may be fragile but he knows where my buttons are and is not above pushing one of them occasionally. I didn't dare point this out, given the state he was in, but that was what I thought when I had a chance to think at all that morning, whether I had an obligation to visit my husband for his son's sake but also whether I could live with myself if something bad did happen to Tim Davis and I hadn't at least stopped by to wish the man well.

I called the hospital on my lunch hour, he's in Roosevelt-St. Luke's in my old neighborhood right next to St. John the Divine's, but all I could get out of the woman I spoke to was that he was in "stable" condition. That's better than critical, although you could be at death's door and be "stable," I figured. But when I called Kevin back I put the best spin on it.

"If he was deteriorating, they'd have him in the ICU," I said, thinking I was telling him good news. But I obviously said the wrong thing or maybe he was just ready to break down anyway, because the next thing I know he's sobbing on the other end of the line. It didn't matter what I said next, he wouldn't stop crying and it finally dawned on me there was only one thing I could say that would make him calm down, and immediately I felt a flash of anger. "All right, I'll go to see him. But just for a minute."

I said I would stop by the hospital after work and give Kevin a call in the evening and in the meantime he should make sure to take his medication and try not to worry, that everything was going to be all right. I barely even heard him when he said goodbye.

I left work half an hour early and walked over to the Broadway local instead of hopping on the "F" train that has a stop just down the block. All during the time I lived with Tim Davis on 121st Street I took that Broadway train virtually every time I went anyplace. I rode it downtown in the morning with the blacks from Harlem and the Jews and Hispanics who live on the Upper West Side. I rode it to Lincoln Center and to the big department stores in midtown until half of them were gone, replaced by cheap discount outlets. I was as familiar with the narrow, damp corridors of its station stops at 72nd, 96th and 110th Streets as any resident of Palookaville, USA is with the cracks in the sidewalks of Main Street.

It all came back to me as I stood hanging onto the metal bar above a dozing cost accountant and his dog-eared copy of the *Wall Street Journal*. The subway cars are no longer the airless cattle wagons of twenty years ago, with lights that flickered on and off and air-conditioning, if there was any, that either froze your ass off or didn't work at all. Even the graffiti is gone, or almost gone, a fad finally like everything else. I was changed too, I told myself, free now to control my own life, no longer defined solely by the man I was married to, free to decide where I go and when, what I will think and free to say so. It wasn't just an illusion, was it, the faux freedom of the chained animal turned loose for a quick romp in the dog run? If not, why was the press of bodies around me making me feel like a farm girl on her first rush-hour subway ride in the big city? Why did I feel like I was on my way to a public execution--my own?

I had been in St. Luke's only once before, the time Kevin broke his arm riding that new bicycle we gave him for his sixth birthday. The place gave me the creeps then and it did the same thing today, though on the inside the hospital was scarcely recognizable from what it was twenty years ago. I rode an elevator with two white-coated men who could have been dressed in SS uniforms as far as I was concerned. Easy does it, I told myself.

Tim Davis was not in isolation, but I had to put on a mask and gown before I was permitted to see him. I didn't mind, I felt almost as if I had been handed a disguise or at least some sort of protection not just against microbes but against my own vulnerability to the man himself. It wasn't enough, of course, not nearly enough, but with the mask across my face I felt as if I could only be half-seen and therefore only half-judged. Even so, as I followed the nurse down the corridor my legs felt as if they each belonged to a different person, someone they couldn't agree about working for, and my chest suddenly seemed made for lungs that were much too small for it. All I needed, I thought, was to pass out and end up in a hospital bed myself, easy prey for Tim Davis sick or not.

"I can only let you have ten minutes," the nurse said possessively, a bit too big in the hips for her tight beige uniform, though Tim Davis never turned up his nose at a little extra female flesh. I pressed my lips together so as not to say something wise-ass in reply.

He had a room to himself, the other bed was unoccupied. There were the usual tubes attached to him, most notably up his nostrils. I didn't see how I was going to have any sort of communication with this person, especially since his eyes were closed. But as soon as I took two steps inside the room they opened and any confidence I still had left dissolved.

"Hi," I said.

He watched me approach to within an arm's length of his bed as if I were some sort of apparition. He had a two-day-old beard that reminded me of the full-length affair he had sported in the sixties and seventies. He looked a bit thinner than he did the morning I squeezed past him in the hallway of our apartment with the last of my belongings in the shopping bags I was carrying, my heart going fast-forward for fear he would divine what I was really up to. Thank

God his mind was on sex at that moment, otherwise, I thought, I might be here today as his still loyal wife.

"How are you feeling?" I said. But he continued to stare at me with the pathetic look of the myopic leery of being duped by this bit of familiar but insubstantial protoplasm hovering nearby. "Dumb question, right?"

I was stretched emotionally about as far I could go. I had imagined this visit in many different scenarios, all of them dreadful. But it never occurred to me that he would put the big freeze on me, he who was not only never at a loss for words but scarcely ever thought it worthwhile to shut up long enough to hear what someone else might have to say. His eyes, I noticed, were a bit glazed, probably from fever, though they looked very much the way they did after he had downed three or four scotches. I figured I had about shot my wad. What did I do next, tell him I would remember him in my prayers? Then his lips started to move in a way that suggested they hadn't been getting much usage in the last few days. He moistened them with the tip of his tongue, swallowed as if it pained him to do so, and tried again. I leaned forward, wondering if I could hear anything through the hiss and whine of the machines attached to him. He said something, but I couldn't make it out, so I came still closer and instinctively put out my hand to lay it on his own where it rested under the sheet. Our faces were just a few feet from each other now. His cracked lips became a tight oval, forming a single word he was unable to pronounce with any force but reached me the same as if he had shouted it.

"Hoor."

XII

I'm a Bad Liar, Too

Wednesday, March 29

Harry called this morning just after I woke up. He sounded awful, I've never heard him like that before. He said he didn't know what had gotten into him, that he didn't believe any of the nasty things he said to me, that he didn't deserve another chance and would never bother me again if I said I didn't want to see him again. He went on for a quarter hour, I was keeping an eye on the time because I had to host a training meeting at nine o'clock and if it went well I might have a shot at getting a better job and finally escape from the smell of dead fish and rancid cooking oil. A couple weeks ago I would have called in sick and run right over to Brooklyn to be with him. I did say, even before he had finished, that of course I would see him again, but a part of me kept her head and realized that if I didn't get out of the job I was in I would be permanently depressed no matter what happened between me and the man in my life. So when the clock showed 7:15 I said why don't we meet for supper.

Ever since I boarded that Broadway local I've felt as if I'm in a time warp and never actually left 121st Street. Seeing Tim Davis after all those weeks of not seeing him at all except for that brief visit he made to my office, the first significant amount of time either of us have spent apart from each other since junior year of high school, has completely turned me upside down. When I left the hospital I scarcely knew who I was or where I was going. For a while I walked aimlessly around the neighborhood, the same patch of city I called home for more than two decades. I know every shop window, practically every vendor along Broadway, at least by sight, from 96th Street all the way up past Columbia University. I felt as if I could easily pop into the Sloane's on 96th Street to pick up something for dinner and then return to the apartment on 121st. I even felt as if a part of me, a much bigger part than I dared admit, wanted to do precisely that, to pretend everything that happened in the last couple months was a daydream or at most a crazy idea that didn't work out, wasn't meant to work out, that my rightful place, my fate, was in Tim Davis's house attending to his needs as best I could and worrying about our son instead of having my fling at freedom. Even when I thought about Harry he seemed no more real than a dream.

It was that "Hoor" that finally brought me back to reality. Had Tim Davis reacted to my visit with a bit more appreciation, had he—and I thank God he didn't—asked for my sympathy or even my love, I don't know what would have happened. At best I would have felt torn between giving him what he wanted and being loyal to the new Deirdre I'd been trying to forge ever since I walked out of his life with a shopping bag clutched in each trembling hand. Luckily, a clock in a laundromat I used to habitually consult during my walks in that neighborhood caught my eye: 5:30. If I didn't get a move on I'd be late meeting Harry, something I had never done before. I'm not one of those women who believe in keeping a man waiting, I've always showed up for any appointment at least ten minutes ahead of time.

I didn't dare tell him where I'd been. I said I had stayed late at the job because of the meeting I attended earlier in the day. I'm a bad liar, I've been told I'm a terrible liar, Harry's even said it himself, not that I ever lie to him, not actually lie, he says I look as if I'm trying to cover up a murder. So even though I could hardly tell him I was with Tim Davis, I shouldn't have said I was at work when I wasn't. Especially since he said, not right away but after we'd had a drink and were waiting for our dinners to arrive, that he called my office at

4:30 and was told I'd already gone for the day. I didn't have it in me to prolong the deception by trying to make up another lie to cover the first, so I told him where I'd actually gone, I was too emotionally spent to do anything else.

"With your husband?" he said, more amazed than angry, I thought, which maybe was a good sign. Only it wasn't, because his voice took on an edge after that, an edge that became sharper with each sentence. Anger, simple outrage even if it meant his causing a scene there in the restaurant, would have been easier to deal with.

"*Ex*-husband," I said.

"What '*ex*'-husband. You've always refer to him as your 'husband.' That's what he is, you're still legally married to him. That's what he'll always be."

"That's not true," I said, but quietly, I didn't want to rile him anymore than he already was.

"How many other times have you been sneaking away to be with him when you told me you were going shopping or working late?"

"He's only been in the hospital two days," I said, not realizing right away that he had something more salacious in mind than a visit to a sickroom.

"Where did the two of you meet? In your old apartment? In a cheap hotel room?"

"I've never been in a cheap hotel room in my life," I said. "I always go first class."

He put down his glass, turned a color very close to purple, I didn't think anyone could actually turn that color, and stood up so fast the entire table almost ended up in my lap.

"Well, good," he said, his face looking so terrible I couldn't stand to look at it, I averted my eyes and no doubt that made me look even more guilty. "Good for you."

I followed him out of the restaurant with a waiter trailing close behind demanding payment for the two drinks we'd had. I had to stop to pay the man, and by that time Harry was a full block away and moving too fast for me to catch up to even if I tried to run after him in my high heels.

I walked all the way to my apartment even though I half-expected Harry to be waiting for me with a gun. I didn't care. I figured I'd screwed up my life so thoroughly now, it would be a relief to have someone blow my brains out for me. Better Harry than some stranger....

I haven't heard from him since, almost a week. I've called his place dozens of times, left scores of messages on his answering machine. When I call him at work he hangs up on me. I wrote him a letter explaining what happened, how Kevin had more or less demanded that I visit his father and how I had to take into consideration the boy's condition. Did he, Harry, think I really wanted to see Tim Davis again? After what he'd put me through? Did he, Harry, think I was such a glutton for punishment that I'd go back for more, or did he, Harry, think I was such a slut that I'd two-time him with the very man I'd left him for, more or less. Did he think no better of me than Tim Davis did?

I wish I'd thought to say these things in the restaurant. But I'm like that, if someone accuses me of anything, anything whatsoever, I assume I'm guilty. If someone yells "Hey, stupid!" on the street I turn around. Writing that letter helped put me on an even keel again, or at least as upright as I ever get. It even made me feel a bit angry for his putting me through yet another ordeal after I'd already been through a pretty emotional afternoon. I wasn't even so sure I wanted to make it up with him if he did apologize. At least not right away. I didn't need this kind of stress in my life, no matter how much I loved him. And I do still love him, and what's worse I can't stand not having him make love to me every day. Whatever he may think about my so-called onanism all I can think about is how good he feels inside me and how much I want him there.

Tuesday, April 4

I got a letter from Lou-Ann. She's coming to New York, some sort of business trip, so we'll finally get to see each other after all these years. I was so happy I dialed her number even before I had my coat off. But I forgot about the time difference between California and New York, so all I got was her answering machine because she was still at work. When I finally did reach her she was on her way to some sort of meeting at her son's high school. I could hardly believe Jason was that old, the last time I'd seen him and his brother they were barely out of diapers. She said she'd call me back when she knew what flight she'll be taking and we could meet for dinner the same night she arrives. I told her she could stay with me if she liked, if she didn't mind sleeping on a portable cot, but she said her agency was paying for a room at the new Marriott opposite Madison Square Garden.

She sounded good, full of the confidence she's always exuded even back when her own marriage, her first marriage, was coming apart. Lou-Ann is a can-do kind of person, something I ascribe to her Yankee upbringing, as if she and her fellow WASPs own this country, so why shouldn't they feel right at home and confident? Both her husbands have been Jewish and both have been named Alan. The first was a sweet but ineffectual guy who seemed intimidated by Lou-Ann's WASPy ways. I liked him a lot, but he got on her nerves, the way he was always deferring to her. Alan, the second Alan, is quiet but not at all shy, and seems much more sure of himself than his predecessor. He even teases Lou-Ann about her Yankee stoicism, something her first husband wouldn't dream of doing....

We met for dinner at her hotel. She looks wonderful, a bit more gray but she always had gray in her hair, even back when we first met at the University of Oregon. I used to envy her gray streaks, I thought they made her look mature and sexy.

She brought me wild sage, she remembers how much I love the vegetation of the California desert where she and her husband vacation. They drive the better part of a day to sit in hot tubs in a desert that regularly reaches 120 degrees in the summertime. I've been a wreck all week, but I didn't want to ruin her stay with my problems, so we talked about her kids and my job, and of course Tim Davis. I told her I'd been to see him in the hospital. "For Kevin's sake. He asked me to."

"How did it go? How did he behave toward you?"

"As per usual. I thought maybe he might act a bit more civil, seeing as how he was so sick, but I was wrong."

I told her what he called me, and she looked so shocked that for a minute I thought she didn't believe it. She always had a good relationship with my husband, "good" in the sense that, while she never approved of his shenanigans, she tried to get me to see them as part of some kind of pathology he suffered from or as the result of his being forced into marriage at too early an age. Once we all turned thirty she no longer made either of these arguments, at least not to my face, but I still sensed she believed I was somehow to blame for his behavior, a "co-dependent," as folks in her line of work like to put it.

"And your gentleman friend? You two are still as blissed out as you were when you wrote me?"

"Not exactly," I said. "I made the mistake of laughing at the wrong time."

"Laughing at what?"

"Well," I said, "at the *wrong* time, if you get my drift. I guess his male ego was offended."

"Deirdre, you didn't."

"I did."

She was looking at me like a schoolmistress whose favorite pupil has just flunked her chemistry final.

"If you could see the contortions we were going through, you might have laughed yourself," I said. "Or maybe not, I don't know. Anyhow, he jumped up and stormed out of the apartment, his own apartment, as it happened. Then, a couple days later he asked if I would have a drink with him, and I said sure, why not. Only, he found out I had just been to see Tim Davis and he went ballistic all over again. Now I don't know if I should even see him again. I mean, I'm as masochistic as the next person, but I'm not looking to end up in a Hefty bag. Not after all I've already been through."

She didn't say anything, she just sat staring at me as if I were some sort of juvenile delinquent or an incorrigible niece she had been asked by the family to give counsel to. I appreciate the fact that she's interested in what I'm going through, God knows I could use some intelligent attention. But what I really need isn't a stern aunt but a friend, or at least someone willing to reserve judgment if she can't wholeheartedly take my side.

We dropped the subject, my life, and talked instead about her own, which was fine with me, though I couldn't help feeling disappointed. I had stupidly imagined some sort of therapy session, with me opening my heart and she offering words of wisdom and comfort. But too much time had passed since we've had that kind of relationship, if we ever actually did. She was, is, willing enough to play big sister but only on the terms an older sibling usually demands. Maybe that's what I wanted at one point in my life, but it's not any longer.

We agreed to meet the next afternoon to go shopping and continue our talk, but I'd already decided that I'd said all I was going to say about anything that mattered to me. When we did meet at Bloomindale's, right around the corner from that dive I stayed in right after I left Tim Davis, I put on a deliberately cheerful manner, "perky" I think they call it in her part of the country. When we said goodbye, with the usual invitation for me to come out and spend a couple weeks with her on the coast, I said I'd love to. But as I walked away to catch the subway back to my apartment, I knew I would probably never see her again.

XIII

I Laugh (but not at) at the Wrong Time

Tuesday, April 11

Kevin's told me his father was released from the hospital this morning. He has some sort of visiting nurse service to look in on him and a home attendant for a few days to cook and clean up. Kevin says he still sounds weak, but that's to be expected, we agreed, and there was none of the resentment I heard in his voice a few days ago. He, Kev, says that he'll be coming east again at Easter, so Tim's illness has turned out to be a boon for me in that respect at least.

"All's well that ends well," I said to Emma after I had given her an edited version of what happened to me in the last week. I was vague at first about what's actually gone on between Harry and myself. I don't know why I didn't lay it all out right from the get-go, I should know by now that Emma will eventually get the full story out of me.

"Sex," she said after I finally told her what the problem was, and then she fell so quiet that I thought I'd grossed her out and even made her regret she ever made friends with me. "Sometimes I wonder if the Almighty didn't invent it in a bad moment, on a bad day, or as a joke."

"I know what you mean," I said. "But I'd be a hypocrite if I said I don't enjoy it. I do, I always have. It's just that they—men, I mean—they have such a different idea from us about what it is."

"Exactly."

"Just when you think you're on the same wavelength, it turns out they're someplace else."

"Or no place at all."

"I didn't mean to imply I wasn't having a good time when Harry got so upset by what I said. I thought he'd see the humor in the situation too. My husband used to make wisecracks all the time. Sometimes I'd be laughing so much I couldn't get back into the swing of things, if you know what I mean."

"Their minds run in different channels. Or puddles, you could say."

"I mean, what's the use if you can't laugh at things, even sex? I didn't mean to insult him as a lover."

"It hurts their ego," she said, a solemn look on her face. I wondered about that "their." I had figured her for a one-man woman, that man being the one who tried to kill both of them but only succeeded in ending his own life. "I had a boyfriend back in my high school days. Tall, dark-haired, big brown eyes. Every time we started kissing, not right away but after we'd been going at it for a while, he'd take my hand, real gently, I thought he was going to kiss it or something, and then instead he put it, you know, down there. Every time he did it I stopped kissing him, and he'd apologize and swear he'd never do it again. And then the next time we kissed he'd do the same thing." She turned toward me with an indignant look, the memory still fresh after all these years. "It wasn't that I didn't want to do what he wanted me to do, it was just that I wanted to do it of my own free will, the same way I was kissing him of my own free will."

"Of course," I said.

"They can be so dense. Eddie was the same way till my accident. No worse, no better. I figured it came with the territory. I really had no cause to complain, he was good as gold in most ways. But, once I was confined to a wheelchair all the ground rules in that regard got turned upside down. Anything that happened after the accident had to start on my own initiative. At least, that was what he thought. Would you believe, Deirdre," she said, her eyes taking on a sparkle as she turned them my way again, "I never had better sex than I did after I'd lost the use of my legs?"

"Really?"

"I kid you not," she said, adding a little nod like a woman with a tasty secret.

"You wouldn't care to go into detail, I suppose."

She turned down the corners of her mouth in an upside-down smile and reached out to pat my hand. "All in due time, my dear."

When I got home who do I find standing outside the entrance to the apartment building but Harry. He looked as if he hadn't slept or taken a bath in days. If I didn't know better I would have taken him for a homeless man, and probably one with psychiatric problems.

"How long have you been here?"

"I was waiting for you to come home from work. But I guess you had someplace else to go."

"I went to see my friend Emma, the paralyzed woman I told you about."

He nodded but I could see he didn't know whether he should believe me, that he wanted to but something kept him from doing so, the same something that made him act crazy in the restaurant that time. "You got my letter?" I said.

He put his hand to the breast pocket of his jacket. My heart gave a jump until I realized what he meant by the gesture was that he had the letter with him.

"Do you really believe I would do you harm?" he said. "Even after what you've put me through?"

"What I've put *you* through? How do you think I felt when you got up and ran out of your apartment? Or when you almost tipped the table into my lap in that restaurant and then went running out into the street like some madman?"

His dark eyes, sunk even deeper into his skull because of the rings beneath them, stared back at me in a confusion of anger and shame.

"How can I carry on a relationship with you," I said, "when I don't know from minute to minute if you're going to go off? I've been nothing but totally faithful to you for all the time we've been together,"—I forgot for the moment about that episode with the man in Sheridan Square, I really had—"and you treat me like I'm the Whore of Babylon."

This was pretty strong talk for somebody who usually let people walk all over her. His expression suddenly became contrite, for a moment I thought he was going to cry.

"I've been walking around Manhattan all day and half of last night," he said. "I couldn't sleep, and I couldn't stand to be in my apartment because you weren't there. I've been walking up and down this block all afternoon, waiting for you to come home."

I didn't know what to say, no one has ever lost any sleep over me, never mind waited an entire afternoon for me just to show up. I put my arms around his chest and held him as tightly as I could. But he didn't hug me back and after a while I let go.

"I'm sorry," he said. "I just can't deal with all of this."

"All of what?"

He shook his head. "All...this," he said with a weak wave toward some sewer repairs going on across the street. "I thought my ego-strengths were better than they are. I didn't think I'd ever get this way again."

"You've been like this before? With someone else?"

He nodded, his eyes lowered to the sidewalk.

"I spent almost ten years in therapy. I spent a fortune. And now here I am going through the same thing all over again."

"It's not your fault," I said, starting to feel the cold, I didn't have one of my warmer coats on.

"Don't make me out to be some kind of monster."

"You're not a monster," I said, my teeth starting to chatter. "Far from it."

"And I'm not a child either. I don't appreciate your patronizing me."

"I'm sorry," I said. "I'm cold and I'm hungry and I've had a long day. At least it seems that way."

"Then, go up to your apartment," he said. "You don't have to stand here talking to me."

"I feel bad. I feel bad that you're walking the streets. I wish you would go home too. I know you don't believe me, but I care about you, Harry."

"I'll be just fine. I have to sort some things out, that's all. I can look out for myself."

"If you need anything... If you need to talk..."

"Go on. Go upstairs to your nice warm apartment."

I tried to kiss him on the cheek, but he pulled away. I could feel him watching me as I entered the building. I didn't known if I was more afraid that he would follow me in or that he wouldn't. This was a Harry I didn't know, a deeply troubled man who dredged up the kind of feelings in me I thought I had left behind on 121st Street. I felt ashamed for being afraid of someone I still loved so much, but my instincts kept telling me to give him a wide berth, that it was only a matter of time before he too would be calling me whore, or something even worse would happen.

When I got upstairs I started to cry out of sheer nervous exhaustion. I went on crying off and on for the rest of the evening. I felt as if a world I had come to feel so secure in, the world Harry and I had shared, was coming apart. I felt worse than I did when I was under Tim Davis's thumb. And it was as if everything I had struggled so hard to gain over the last few months had no value now, that I would live and die a lonely, unloved woman.

The phone rang at 9:00 p.m., but there was no one on the line when I answered. It rang again an hour later, and again at 11:00.

XIV

I Might as Well be Dead

Thursday, April 13

Did I mention I gave up smoking? Two weeks ago. Harry talked me into it, though I didn't need much talking, I'm not stupid, I know what it does to my lungs and heart. The funny thing is, I didn't miss them, at least not much. Whenever I got a craving, I just made love with Harry and that would make the craving go away.

Now I'm back on them. I started the day Harry walked out of his apartment leaving me naked in his bed. If we had made up I would have stopped again, but I can't live without Harry and without cigarettes. I didn't smoke when we met for dinner the other night because I knew how much my giving up cigarettes meant to him. Not just for health reasons but because he knew that being with him gave me the strength to do without them. Seeing me with a cigarette in my mouth would have been like his seeing me in the arms of another man.

But now I have no reason not to smoke, apart from its killing me. It's not the nicotine I crave, at least that's not how it seems. When I have a lit cigarette in my hand I feel I'm not alone, like I have a friend, someone I can turn to who will always be there for me. When I gave them up, and I've done it before, for almost a year when I was seeing Forrest, I only did so when I had something more powerful to take their place.

Now I sit on the bare floor of my living room and smoke one cigarette after another. I keep hoping Harry will call, not the crazy Harry of the last week but the loving man whose love and attention I've come to rely on so much. I feel like half of me is missing and all the cigarettes in the world can't fill that void. I keep trying to figure out what it is about me that turns men into overbearing bastards like Tim Davis or makes them crazy like Harry. And I feel so bad for him, because I can see how much he's suffering. Only, I don't know what I can do about it without exposing myself to more abuse, and I won't do that, I just can't do that anymore, not after enduring more than twenty years of it from my husband.

I feel a little better when I talk to Emma. But from the way she looks at me I sometimes wonder if she doesn't think I'm just as crazy as the men in my life do. I am crazy, I know that already, I've always known that, and I suppose I should go and see a therapist like Harry suggested. But I hate doctors or anyone like doctors, including therapists, lawyers, accountants, any kind of professional. They're all so goddamn smug and they always make me feel like I'm just a kid and they're not, while all the time they're either playing with themselves or thinking about it.

I've had a couple drinks. Half a bottle of red wine, in fact, so I probably sound a little disjointed, more than usual, I mean. If I'm not careful I'll end up an alcoholic and homeless, living out of a cardboard box on 42nd Street, only I can't do that because what will become of Kevin? I have to hold myself together for his sake. Only, sometimes I need to kill the ache inside me, or at least dull it, and a few glasses of wine help. I'll have a headache in the morning—how come I never got hung over when Harry and I drank, and we got pretty blotto sometimes?--but I don't care, the job I have doesn't require a clear head, doesn't require any head at all, actually, an ape could do it.

I never thought I'd end up like this. I was going to have a real career, not like my Aunt Rose who got herself a law degree and then spent the rest of her life behind a cash register in her husband's butcher shop and looking after his three bastards from a previous marriage. Then I met Tim Davis, which would have been okay, I still would have gone on to college and graduate school, only for my getting pregnant. Why did I have to get pregnant? It's not as if we weren't taking precautions. If I had only had some intelligent parenting, some direction, the attention I needed, access to an abortion. But that's all history now. I did get pregnant, I didn't have an abortion, and here I am twenty-some years later, forty years old, no man in my life, a shitty job, all alone in an underheated apartment, the new super is tight as a crab's ass about sending up steam. I might as well be dead.

Saturday, April 15

As if I didn't have enough on my mind, my mother called first thing this morning and told me she has diabetes. My head was still throbbing from all the wine I'd drunk last night, I finish the better part of a bottle every night now. The radiator was banging like it was possessed, I thought Ed Cleary had fixed it once and for all, but I guess not. And now this.

"It showed up during a regular exam," she said in her usual emotionless tone, as if it were someone else she were talking about, some distant relative she never much cared for anyway. I asked how she could be so damned cool about it. I wouldn't have been in such a belligerent mood except I half-believed she was calling me on a Saturday morning with this happy news because she somehow knew the state I was in. "One has to put up with these things, my dear," she said. "There's no sense trying to fight fate."

This was just more of the same pseudo-stoicism she had picked up during her year at the Sorbonne and pretended to live by for as long as I've known her. I asked how she felt and what sort of treatment she would be getting. She said what she had was late-onset diabetes, the least serious kind, and all she would have to do is watch her diet carefully and have her blood tested from time to time.

"I'm not getting any younger, Deirdre. I know I can't live forever. I'm resigned to whatever destiny has in store for me."

"You'll probably outlive me," I said. "Though that isn't saying much anymore."

She asked whatever did I mean, I was a lovely young woman with my whole life ahead of me. But this morning, whether it was my pounding head or the throbbing radiator, I wasn't in a mood for her clichés. I told her I'd just lost the man I loved and didn't know if it was my fault or not, that my ex-husband had called me a whore from what might have turned out to be his deathbed, and my only friend was a woman who tried to commit suicide just a couple weeks ago.

My outburst gave her pause, but not much. Predictably, she picked up on what I had said about her son-in-law. "He was seriously ill? How did you find out?" She never even alluded to the word he had spoken to me—the *only* word, I made a point of reminding her. "He's a sick man," she replied ambiguously. "You can't take seriously what he says."

She didn't know the half of it, but she wouldn't want to hear yet another complaint from me about what a bully her wonderful Tim was. "Kevin was in town for a visit," I told her in order to change the subject before I said something I might regret. The sun rose and set on her grandson. "We went to the library on 42nd Street. They had an exhibition of Dickens' manuscripts. You know how he loves Dickens."

"How is my darling boy?" she said. "He looked so thin the last time I saw him."

We chatted for a while about the one topic in which we shared a genuine mutual interest, then she asked, "What are you planning to do, Deirdre? Are you thinking of getting a divorce?"

"I imagine I am," I said. "That's what everyone keeps telling me I should do. I just don't fancy having to fight Tim Davis in court. You know he'll contest it."

"You should end it, my dear, if you have no intention of going back to him. End it and be done with it."

"Easy for you to say. You don't have to stand before a judge and hear your husband hold forth about what a dirty little tart you've been. Besides, I'm not especially fond of courtrooms and judges, and you may remember why."

But she didn't take the bait, she never does. Avoid a scene at any cost, is her motto. Bury the past along with your head in the sand. Instead, she told me I know best, it's my life.

"You know, Mother, I realize you've had a bit of a shock with this diabetes thing, but I've got to tell you, I could use a little moral support at this point in my life. I didn't put up much of a stink when you and Daddy decided to move to Florida when I could have used your help with Kevin, not to mention the crap I had to put up with from Tim Davis. But you said Daddy needed to be in a warmer climate, so I didn't object, not really. And I haven't troubled you much over the years since then with my problems, and I've had some problems, I can tell you."

I was getting teary at this point. Ordinarily I'd squelch it, my mother gets embarrassed when someone cries. But this morning for some reason I decided not to, either in the hope she would find it in herself to offer some real sympathy or maybe just to lay some of the burden I'd been bearing alone for all these years at her doorstep where some of it belonged.

"All I ask," I said, "is that you pay a little attention, show just a... modicum of concern." Sniff, sniff. "It's not as if you have another child besides me. Is it so difficult, after all? Don't you care about what happens to me, what I'm going through?"

There was a pause on the other end of the line, a pause and a deep breath.

"Of course I care, Deirdre," she said as if she were reading the words off a page. "I can't imagine how you could ever imagine otherwise. I care about you, and I care about what you're going through."

"Then, why doesn't it feel like you do? Why does it feel like you're just going through the motions? Even when I was a little kid, when I came running to you for a hug after I scraped my knee, you didn't take me on your lap like other mothers did. You just told me not to worry, the pain would go away if I just thought about something else."

"I don't remember saying any such thing."

"Well, I do. You don't forget things like that. Anything, just so you didn't have to get involved, so you wouldn't have to put yourself out."

"Really, Deirdre, you're not making any sense at all, my dear."

"All you cared about was your friends at the Russian Tea Room.

You couldn't get away from me and Daddy fast enough, like we were poor relations you were ashamed of."

"I don't have to listen to this Deirdre. I don't care how distraught you may be about your marriage breaking up."

"I'm *not* distraught about my marriage breaking up. If you really had been listening, you'd know I'm upset because Harry, the man I love, is acting like a nut job all of a sudden. *Harry*, Mother, not Tim Davis. There's a difference. Tim Davis can drop dead tomorrow, for all I care. *You* may care about Tim Davis, but I don't. It's Harry I'm worried about. H-A-R-R-Y, Harry."

"You're very upset, I can hear that in your voice. But I really don't think you can lay all your troubles at my doorstep. Your father and I always acted in what we believed was your best interest. But you had a mind of your own, as they say. I don't blame you for that. I..."

At that point I started crying so hard I couldn't hear what she was saying. I rarely cry in the presence of my mother. I cried when I found out I was pregnant and when she told me she and my father were moving to Florida, and the day my father was buried. Each time, she merely looked at me as if I were a stranger throwing some sort of tantrum. Not a word and certainly not any gesture of sympathy, much less a hug. Even now as I let the sobs come unchecked, I pictured her sitting with the phone half an inch from her ear so she wouldn't have to hear my sniffling and wheezing, she hates any kind of mouth or nose noises. But I made no effort to get hold of myself.

"My life is going down the toilet, and I have no one, no one, not a single person to turn to."

"That's not true, Deirdre. I'm here for you, I really am. I'm sorry if I don't say it the way you want me to. I do the best I can. You have to make allowances."

I wanted to believe her so badly that I suspended my disbelief. Now I know what people who turn to religion in times of crisis feel like. When there's nothing else around, you grab for whatever is available and pray it's not just an illusion.

"You're all I have left in this world, my dear. Not that you weren't the light of my life even before your father passed away. But I had to attend to his needs. I was his wife. If the choices had been mine entirely, don't you think I might have acted differently?"

I wasn't sure what she was referring to, the move to Florida was the obvious possibility. But her words set off a number of other possibilities: the way she handled or chose not to handle my pregnancy, not to mention my entire childhood and adolescence; the court case against Tim Davis; plus dozens of lesser crises that had come up over the years when I turned to her, or tried to turn to her.

"Are you saying you did everything you did in the way you did it because that's the way Daddy wanted you to?"

"Not in every case. But I had to take his opinions very much into account, didn't I. Not that he also didn't think the world of you, Deirdre. If anything, he sinned by being overly fond. And for a man like him, someone of his generation, that meant trying to be as protective as he could, shielding you from the bad things of the world. He didn't go about it in quite the same way as I would have, but I had to respect how he felt, especially because I knew how much he loved you."

There it was, that word again. All I had to do was hear it to start the tears flowing.

"Oh dear, did I say the wrong thing again?"

"No," I said. "For once you said the right one."

XV

I Remember Sarah

Thursday, April 20

When I was a kid I used to wake up at night and hear noises in our kitchen, pans being moved around on the stove, dishes and glasses clinking. I thought it was a burglar who had taken time out from his burglarizing to make himself scrambled eggs. I was too afraid to get up and go out to my parents' sofa-bed in the living room, I would have had to pass right by the kitchen and be spotted by the intruder. So I just lay there, listening to what I thought were the muted sounds of the frying pan and spatula. I never told either my mother or father what I heard. I did mention it once to Sarah, our maid and baby-sitter, but she just laughed and told me I had a wonderful imagination.

Lately I've been waking up and hearing those same sounds. I know there's no one in my kitchen, much less someone fixing himself scrambled eggs before making off with my costume jewelry. But I swear that's what it sounds like, and just as I used to lie in bed too terrified to move thirty years ago, I lay now hiding under the covers on my sofa-bed. At any moment I expect the burglar to be done with his meal and then have another look around the apartment and maybe spot me cowering under the covers, and who knows what he'll do then, wring my neck at the very least.

I told Emma about my fantasy the other day, and she said she used to hear an animal rooting around under her bed, a porcupine or opossum, she thought, even though she's never seen either of those animals in real life. She was afraid that if she let herself drift off to sleep the animal would eat her toes.

"Did you tell your parents?" I said.

"I was afraid to. I thought they'd think I was imagining things and put me away."

"'Put you away'?"

"Like they did Cathy Farrell, the retarded girl who lived on the next floor. Her parents put her in an institution when she was hardly more than an infant. They would bring her home at Christmas or Thanksgiving. Just for a few hours. I thought that's how I would end up if I opened my mouth about the animals under my bed. It's funny how a kid's mind works."

I didn't think it was funny at all, especially since my own mind is working now the same way it did when I was six.

"You're just under a lot of stress, what with your boyfriend treating you the way he's done, and your husband. You should try to get away, take a vacation. It would do you good. When was the last time you took a trip?"

"I went out to the coast to visit my friend Lou-Ann six years ago."

"Didn't you and your husband ever go away?"

"Not hardly. How about you?"

"All the time. I mean, whenever we could afford it. I loved to travel, before the accident, that is. I love the great outdoors, especially the western part of the United States."

"I remember your husband saying that." She looked at me carefully, as if I had just reported some intimate detail of her married life. "He mentioned it when I was signing the lease for my apartment, down in his basement office. He said how much you liked the American West. I think he even said you were planning to take a trip out there."

"He said that?"

"I'm pretty sure he did," I said, thinking maybe it wasn't such a good idea, my bringing up her recent past. "I didn't mean to stir up bad memories."

We talked about something else. There's always something to talk about with Emma. She's interested in everything, not just personal stuff but politics, books she's read or would like to read, stories about the other people in the nursing home. It's remarkable how she can keep a sense of humor about her situation. If it was me, they'd have to put me in a strait jacket to keep me from absconding or at least biting someone. But Emma just takes it all in stride. I sometimes think she could find herself in even worse circumstances and not lose her sense of humor. They say some people were like that in the Nazi camps, there's a whole genre called Holocaust jokes that Jews only tell each other, they're so gruesome. I picture Emma as one of those blest or maybe just crazy people who go on making wisecracks right up to the moment they get shoved into an oven. Not me, I'd be scratching and clawing. Either that or I'd find a way to do away with myself before the bastards had a chance to kill me themselves.

Emma and I still haven't talked about one particular topic, though, what actually happened the night her husband took his life. Whenever she makes any reference to his death, however obliquely, she talks as if he had a heart attack or got run over by a bus. No hint of suicide, much less a suicide pact. I don't know if she really believes he died a natural death or if she's hiding the truth from herself, has convinced herself it didn't happen like that. I've thought any number of times how awful it must have been for her to wake up in St. Vincent's and discover her husband had killed himself and not taken her with him, if that was what they really planned. Some day, I figure, I'll learn the truth, but for now I just play along.

Meanwhile, I haven't heard from Harry in more than a week and I'm up to two packs of cigarettes a day. I figure at this rate I'll be dead from emphysema in a year. Small loss, except for Kevin, I don't want to leave him in the lurch, he doesn't really have anyone else unless you count his crazy father. Tim Davis writes him long-winded epistles about how Kev is reaping the fruits of his own folly—just what the boy needs to hear. At least Tim's stopped writing to my mother.

Kevin has also heard from Sarah, my mother's maid who also looked after Kevin now and then when he was young. She had become part of the family by then and did a better job of caring for him than I ever did. I gladly turned him over to her when my mother was busy with her friends when I was going out of my mind changing diapers and studying for a college degree at the same time. Sarah would hop a subway up to the Bronx from Harlem, take charge of the one-bedroom apartment in the project where Tim Davis and I were living and tell me to go to the library and do my schoolwork. She never had any formal education herself beyond a few years of elementary school, but she believed passionately in education and probably would have worked for nothing if it helped me get my degree. Her own sons are both professionals, an accountant and a lawyer. A third boy died young from a drug overdose. He was the same age as myself, sixteen or seventeen. I was in the midst of my pregnancy when he died and scarcely able to think about anything but what had happened to me, though I did notice that all of a sudden Sarah didn't seem her cheerful self. When my mother told me what had happened I was shocked but almost as if she had told me Sarah's old dog had died. I never met any of Sarah's children, a remarkable fact when you think how intimately her life was tied up with my own.

She worked for us, technically for my mother but also for me in reality, for the better part of thirty years. She is there among my first conscious memories right through the last days of Kevin's senior year of high school. She attended his graduation just as she had attended his graduation from elementary and junior high, just as she had been present at my own school functions right from kindergarten up through my graduation from CCNY. She baked the cake for my ersatz wedding reception, an "intimate affair" for just my parents, Tim Davis's family and a few friends. She held my hand when the contractions started a few months later and insisted on changing the baby's diapers when I came home from the hospital.

I probably haven't seen her more than half a dozen times in the last decade. Kevin never fails to visit her when he's in town. He took a side trip up to 155th Street where she lives when he came to visit me, though I didn't think it worth mentioning, did I. The truth is I have very ambivalent feelings toward Sarah (her real name is Sarie, but my mother always insisted we call her Sarah). She was as responsible for my upbringing as my mother was, if the amount of time I spent with her counts for anything. Some of my earliest memories are of sitting on her lap, listening to her deep Southern voice read nursery rimes or Bible stories. She was especially fond of the story of Abraham and Isaac and the way God ordered Abraham to sacrifice his only-begotten son, but then relented at the last moment and gave Abraham a ram to sacrifice instead. Later on, I came to despise that story. What sort of God would pull a cheap trick like that on someone who was as devoted to him as Abraham was? But when I was very young I listened enthralled, just as I did to all the other tales and poems she read to me, including Little Black Sambo and the Uncle Remus Tales, which she laughed over, a big belly-shaking laugh that made me bounce up and down on her lap, a sensation I came to love as much as being pushed on the swings—better, since I never feared flying off her lap the I way I feared falling from the cold slippery seats of the swings in the nearby park she took me to.

I don't understand why I came to resent Sarah, if "resent" is the word. I don't know how to explain why I virtually shunned her once I no longer needed her to help me look after Kevin. I've never given the subject much thought until the last couple weeks, when I've had nothing but time to think, it seems, think and smoke cigarettes. Sarah used to scold me for my smoking, especially since I refused to give it up when I was pregnant. She told me I would give the baby bad lungs, an idea I knew to be fanciful, though it turned out she was right about smoking being harmful to a fetus in other ways, we know that now. I suppose to some extent I took her for granted.

But there's more to it than that, something stronger and more negative, a sense of some sort of wrong having been done me, though I still can't for the life of me understand what, unless it was because she did in fact take the place of my mother so often, not just when I was a child but also when I was starting to raise my own offspring. I should go and visit her, pay my respects, she's just a short subway ride away. Kevin has her telephone number, they talk on the phone regularly. That's how she found out about me and Tim Davis breaking up. Kevin even said she would like to see me. Only,

I'm afraid she'll blame me for the breakup, she's always taken my husband's side, women always do. Tim's probably told her about my infidelities, few as they've been, without of course mentioning his own, though they wouldn't count as heavily against him as mine do against me because he's a man, after all, and they're not supposed to be able to control themselves. I don't look forward to hearing another lecture about my duties as a wife and mother, especially since I wouldn't dare tell Sarah to fuck off the way I would somebody else.

XVI

My Goose Gets Overcooked

Tuesday, May 2

I miss Harry. Not just the obvious things, having him inside me, having his hard body pressed against my own. I miss his lying beside me, his breathing, the scary way he pauses after each long inhale when he's asleep. I miss his goofy look when he wakes up in the morning. I miss his smell and the way he eats. I miss him, I just do.

I called him this evening, but there was no answer. The first time I just hung up, but on the second try I left a message. I told him how I feel, how I don't care what he says or does, how I don't want to live the rest of my life without him. Lou-Ann would say I'm looking for trouble. Emma would stare at me in silent amazement, or maybe not, I don't care. I can wither up and die from my own misery or I can go down in flames with Harry if that's my fate. I'll take that chance, it's no contest as far as I'm concerned. I'm not me without him. I'm not anything and, coward that I am, I don't want to live at all if I can't have him in my life.

I waited up till almost two a.m. to see if he would return my call. I didn't sleep much after that. Now it's seven in the morning and I haven't even begun to dress for work. This is bad. I can take one or two days off, but if I don't pull myself together one way or the other

I'm going to end up losing my job and then my apartment and finally I'll be living in a cardboard box outside Grand Central Station.

Sometimes I wonder what it is with me and men, the few men I've actually had anything to do with. I don't like to think there's some kind of pattern there. They say most of us just keep repeating the same relationship, no matter how many different lovers we have in our life. I'm not so much of a fool that I can't see some of that is true. My father was a domineering man, so was Tim Davis. I guess Harry is too, though in a very different way from Tim or my father.

What I mean is, I seem to relate to men in a very different way than other women do. I like men, and I don't think other women do, not really. There's a lot of talk about how men trash women, "objectify" them in their locker-room, bar-stool buddy talk. But women do the same thing, in spades. Women are as crude as any man. The difference is, or is supposed to be, that women have got the shorter end of the stick historically, so they have a right to scheme and connive. It's like the so-called race issue: Blacks can't be racists because they're the oppressed. That's a lot of crap, if you ask me. I'm always amazed at the raw hatred women bear toward the opposite sex, and I'm talking married heterosexual women. They put on one face for their men, then behind their backs talk about them like they're the scum of the earth. Women of all ages. I first came across this in the parks when Kevin was just a toddler. Twenty-year-olds with a good life, money in the bank, they would sit and bitch for hours about things I never would discuss with a close friend, never mind strangers. Like what losers their men were in bed compared with other guys they'd slept with. Or how disgusting their husbands' eating habits were. I couldn't believe my ears. Now I take it for granted. Women like Emma are the exception. Like me, she genuinely likes men, not just sexually but as people. Or at least we don't *dis*-like them.

None of which helps much in my current relationship, or what's left of it. I'm used to a man trying to lord it over me, not one who goes to pieces if I look at him the wrong way. This is all virgin territory and I don't know how to handle it. All I know is that without Harry I feel like someone's cut out half my insides but I go on living somehow just the same.

I'm tired of thinking. It's all I do. And now I've started talking to myself as well. I didn't notice at first because I kind of complain out loud about things anyway even when there's nobody around. But this morning I realized I was having whole conversations with myself, one-sided, of course, I'm not that loony yet. I was thinking about something that happened ten years ago, a Christmas dinner with Tim Davis and Kevin. I always cooked a turkey for Christmas, though every year I begged for a goose. As a kid we never celebrated Christmas, not the way gentiles did, with a tree and midnight mass, or whatever Protestants do. Dickens was my source for Christmas customs, and they always ate a goose for Christmas in his stories. Kevin took my side and asked for a goose too, but his father said a turkey had more meat and was more practical, so every year we ended up having turkey, a frozen one we bought at the last minute from Sloane's or Gristedes or whatever store was open late on Christmas Eve when we did most of our Christmas shopping, including for the tree and most of the presents.

But one year I got my wish. I still don't know why my husband relented, but that Christmas he said okay, I could have my goose. He probably figured it was time to teach me a lesson. So, instead of one of us running out for the usual frozen turkey, I was allowed to try to find—it must have been ten o'clock on Christmas Eve--a goose. I actually found a butcher store still open that had one that was fresh, never-frozen. It was a monster, twelve pounds or more. I had to lug it back to the apartment all by myself, along with fixings for stuffing, gravy and probably ten pounds of potatoes for the sweet-potatoes-with-marshmallows Kevin loved.

Usually I slept late on Christmas morning while Tim Davis took Kevin to mass and a walk around the neighborhood. But that year I was up at the crack of dawn. I dug out the copy of *The Joy of Cooking* my Aunt Bella gave me when I got married and read up on the preparation of goose. It didn't seem much different from cooking a turkey, as far as I could see, so I popped it into our tiny oven and prayed the temperature I set it for would end up being within fifty degrees of what was required.

After Kevin opened his presents, usually a couple books from his father and something more appropriate to an adolescent boy from me, such as a baseball mitt, the wrong size or position, of course, he and his father turned on a football game and settled down in the living room to wait for the goose to be done. Every once in a while my husband poked his nose into the kitchen and asked with a smirk how it was doing. I told him to piss off. About the only time I ever stood up on my hind legs was when I was trying to do something I really found difficult, like cooking, and he would offer advice or, more likely, criticism.

"You want to cook it yourself, be my guest," I remember telling him at one point even though he hadn't actually said anything, just stood there in the kitchen doorway looking amused at my struggles. "Otherwise stay the fuck out of here."

He seemed to enjoy my irritability, though at the time I didn't realize why. If he had insisted on coming into the kitchen and showing me the right way to cook a goose, I probably would have capitulated and let him, even though I would have felt like screaming. But if I turned on him it wasn't unusual for him to try to get me to come into the bedroom. And I did, more than once, never putting two and two together, that it was my back talk that was turning him on. To me his amorous moments were always unpredictable and mysterious, it's only looking back I can see how they corresponded with moments when I found him irritating to be around.

Anyway, about two hours into the baking that goose began to smoke like a four-alarm fire, I had no idea how fatty they were. At first I couldn't imagine what was causing all the smoke, the kitchen was full of it even after I opened two or three windows. I yelled for Tim to come and help, but he only stood in the doorway again, smirking while I cursed and opened more windows. Soon the neighbors began noticing the smoke pouring out of our apartment and then we heard fire engines on the street outside. I had no idea they were for us until the firemen began rapping on the door with their big fists. Tim answered it and pointed them toward the kitchen. All of a sudden two big lugs in slickers were standing next to me with axes in their hands.

"Better step outside, lady," one of them says. The other produces a fire extinguisher that looked like it should take two men to carry, opened up my oven door and pointed it at my innocent goose. There was no fire in there, I knew that already, but he shot white foam into the oven until it was spilling out onto the kitchen floor. Only then did he reach in and pull out the goose, at this point just about fully cooked, though of course covered in foam. He put it into the sink next to the stove, then shot some more foam into the oven.

By now I had recovered from the shock of finding two fully armed firemen in my kitchen and realized they had just ruined my Christmas dinner.

"You fucking idiot!" I yelled.

The young fireman didn't even turn my way, but his partner who was standing by just in case the goose tried any funny business said, "Lady, we ain't here to save nobody's dinner."

"But it wasn't on fire! It was just smoking. It's a goddamn goose!"

"Can't take no chances, lady."

Meanwhile, Tim Davis was standing just behind me with Kevin who didn't have a clue to what was going on. I assumed Tim must be as outraged as I was, it was his dinner that was just ruined as well as my own. He managed to keep something like a straight face until the firemen finished their work, then offered them a beer, which they declined, and saw them to the door, clapping one of them on the shoulder. Have I mentioned that Tim Davis is a cop groupie? Well, now I found out he was a firemen groupie as well. Anything in uniform.

Meanwhile, I was fuming almost as much as the oven had been. My goose was ruined, the only one I'd ever had a chance to make. No Dickens Christmas for us, with Kevin sitting there like Tiny Tim and his father playing Scrooge and Bob Crotchet combined.

"We'll get some Chinese takeout," my husband said, as if this were an ordinary Sunday afternoon instead of Christmas Day.

"*You'll* get Chinese takeout," I said, pulling off the little apron I had put on for the occasion—ordinarily I'd no more wear an apron than I would a pair of handcuffs. I was in tears and too upset even to think about how poor Kevin was taking all this. I stomped into our bedroom and locked the door behind me.

Kevin stood outside the bedroom door after his father had gone back to watch his football game—or, more likely, read a book, the football game was just a bit of camp, he hated sports as much as I

did. "Mother?" Kev kept saying. "Are you all right, Mother?" I didn't
answer. He and his father were one to me at the moment, and I despised them both for ruining my Christmas dinner. I even suspected
Tim had called the fire department himself, that would have been his
idea of a joke. After a while Kevin stopped tapping on the bedroom
door. Then I thought I heard the apartment door open and close,
it made a distinctive squeak and groan no matter how slowly you
opened or closed it. I waited another ten minutes, then got up to
make sure they had indeed gone out, probably to get that Chinese
takeout which I still had no intention of sharing.

Sure enough, they had left. I pulled on my winter coat, the one
that made me look like a Michelin tire, but didn't bother putting on
the boots I always wear throughout the winter months and even well
into the spring, I hate the cold. Then I let myself out of the apartment and snuck down the stairs because I knew Kevin and his father
would be taking the elevator. When he was younger Kevin loved to
push the buttons and pretend he was an elevator operator and the
other tenants in the building usually played along.

It was bitter cold outside, no sunshine, just a dead gray sky. I
headed down 121st Street in the opposite direction from Broadway to
avoid running into Kevin and his father, then doubled back toward
Riverside Park. I'm not much for taking walks in winter, I've already
said how I hate the cold, but I'd had it with Tim Davis. I wouldn't
have minded so much if I had ruined the goose myself and he had
mocked me at the dinner table. I mean, I *would* have minded, but not
the way I did about what actually happened. That goose meant a lot
to me. I can't begin to explain why. I wouldn't have begged for one
every year if it didn't. And then to see it destroyed by firemen while
Tim Davis stood laughing up his sleeve, that was too much, just
more than I could bear, even a masochistic wimp like me.

There were plenty of people out in the park, dog-walkers and
Jews who would be eating Chinese food themselves and going to
one of the movies on Broadway, a Christmas ritual almost as traditional for them as it was for Christians to stay at home with family
and eat a big feast. I used to feel sorry for them because they didn't
have someplace to go on Christmas, and considered myself lucky
that I did, that I didn't have to pretend it didn't matter that none of

my gentile friends cared to invite me to their house to see their tree and exchange presents. I always felt sorry for Jews on Christmas because I assumed they felt like I did, that they would give their eye teeth to have a tree and sit around listening to Bing Crosby and Nat Cole sing Christmas songs. I knew they had their seders, but I'd been to a few seders in my time and they didn't compare with Christmas. It didn't matter that I'd never actually had a Christmas like that myself. My husband would no more listen to Bing Crosby sing "White Christmas" than he would go to a Friday-night Shabbos service. My idea of Christmas wasn't one I actually had experienced but the holiday I had fixed in my imagination like a pimple that wouldn't go away, the Christmas of the commercials on TV where everyone can't wait to get home to their "loved ones," the Christmases of the sentimental sitcoms I had grown up on and all those Perry Como specials. That was what Tim Davis had ruined for me, never mind that it wasn't he but the stupid firemen who actually destroyed my goose. And that was what I just couldn't accept, no matter how many other humiliations and abuses I'd accepted during the ten years I'd been living with him.

I wandered south until I reached that section somewhere in the nineties where you can always find tourists taking in the view of New Jersey, along with the usual joggers and old duffers from the neighborhood. There weren't any tourists that afternoon, at least nothing as obvious as a klatch of Japanese and their cameras or oil sheiks with their girlfriends. There was just me and an elderly woman who was feeding the pigeons.

I put my elbows up on the thick stone wall and stared across the Hudson at some apartment buildings on the other side. A lone tugboat was steaming upriver, scarcely making any headway. It seemed a futile effort it was putting forth, when everyone else but me and this old woman were at home watching football or sleeping off a big midday meal.

I heard somebody say something but assumed it wasn't meant for me until I heard it again. When I turned around there was still no one there except the old woman, but she was smiling like one of those old women on Broadway when they seem to be zoning out and reliving something that happened forty years earlier.

"I said, had a tiff with your boyfriend?"

I don't ordinarily talk to strangers, even female strangers, but this one didn't exactly look like she was packing a Saturday-night-special under her black goose-down coat.

"Not exactly," I said.

She kept on throwing pieces of bread a few at a time at the horde of pigeons gathered at her feet, I would no more feed a pigeon than I would a rat, her thin mouth still creased with that dreamy smile, the same one my mother put on when she used to take me window shopping on Fifth Avenue and some stranger in a smart double-breasted suit would tip his hat and wish her a good day. I used to wonder about that smile.

"I thought you looked like you had a tiff, that's all. It's none of my business," she said, tossing another handful of bread at the greedy pigeons. "I was just thinking to myself, that girl's had a row with her beaux on Christmas Day."

"Actually, it was more like a fight, and it was with my husband."

"Oh," she said, raising her thin, heavily penciled eyebrows, she still hadn't looked directly at me. She was wearing high calfskin boots, and there were rings on her hand that didn't come from Woolworth's basement. "Your husband," she said. "That's different."

"He let the firemen ruin my goose," I said, moving as close as I dared to the filthy flock at her feet. "Ruined my Christmas dinner."

"Is that right? Your goose was on fire?"

"No, it wasn't. It was just smoking a lot. Ten years I've been asking him to let me have a goose for Christmas, and then he goes and ruins it."

"I see," she said, looking around to see who else might be about, just in case. "Well, maybe he'll let you have another."

"I don't want another. That was it. That was my one chance to have a goose for Christmas."

She gave a little shrug under her goose down, emptied the last crumbs from the plastic bag that held the pigeon's food, then brushed her hands vigorously against each other to clean them.

"My husband used to love duck," she said. "We didn't celebrate Christmas, so anytime was a good time for him to have it. Mostly he ordered it when we ate out, but a couple times I made it at home for him. Glazed in cherry sauce and wine, or maybe vermouth, I don't remember now. Much too fatty to my taste, but he said he enjoyed it."

"My mother made duck once in a while. Is it anything like goose?"

"Actually," she said, her face brightening the way rich people's faces do when certain subjects come up in conversation, usually money. But the change in her expression made her look twenty years younger, younger and elegant, the way I'd like to look in twenty-five or thirty years. "Actually, come to think of it, they are quite a bit alike. All dark meat, you know. That's why they're so fatty. You have to be careful not to overcook or undercook."

"Well, I guess I'll never know."

"Don't be silly," she said. "You can't let this one bad experience defeat you."

"Nope," I said, "this was my one shot. I should have known it would end up a disaster. Most things I try usually do."

"Oh, my. I think we're upset about something besides a goose."

I didn't say anything. I knew she could see the tears in my eyes, I was hoping she wasn't nearsighted. She hesitated--I might have been some loony after all, one thing you do not do in New York is trust strangers—but then said, "Would you like to walk a bit? I thought I'd head over to the Old Vienna for a cup of something hot. Perhaps you'd care to join me?"

XVII

Coffee and Sympathy

The Same Day

I hadn't been in the Old Vienna since my mother took me there fifteen years ago. But it hadn't changed a bit. The plush banquettes, the old-world crystal. The waiters were younger, in my mother's day they were all European immigrants, refugees from the Nazis. The woman who showed me and Edith—she didn't tell me her last name—to a small table covered in thick white cloth, could have been Russian, Hispanic or neither of those, I couldn't tell.

"They changed hands about ten years ago," Edith said with the look of someone for whom such information had more than a passing interest. "Order whatever you like, my dear. I'm just having coffee. They make an excellent cheesecake—but of course you know that already."

In some ways she reminded me of my mother. There was the same elegant manner and ease around waiters and servants in general. Such women seem only to properly exist when they're ensconced in an expensive restaurant perusing an oversize menu. Even after my father died, my mother seemed to become a different person when she took me and Kevin out for lunch at one of her favorite watering holes. Sometimes the waiter or maitre d' recognized her, and the way she acknowledged his greeting, a delicate balance of pleasure and condescension, impressed me no end.

"I didn't mean to get carried away," I said. "It's just that today's been an especially bad day for me, or maybe you're such a good listener I couldn't help myself. You probably have better things to do with your time."

"Don't be silly, my dear. I have absolutely nothing better to do. Nobody invites an old widow like myself to their house, least of all on Christmas Day. Besides, I haven't had anything to eat today but a bowl of Wheaties."

By now, I assumed that Kevin and my husband had returned from wherever it was they had slipped out to when I was sulking in the bedroom. They would wonder where I went off to, but not for long. At least, not Tim Davis. Kevin would worry, he still worries about everything, takes after me in that regard. But he would find something to amuse himself, and his father would dig out one of his books about medieval theology. They knew I'd be back, I always came back.

"Have you ever thought of leaving him?" Edith asked, putting a thick layer of butter onto a small but dense-looking sweet roll. "I used to consider leaving my own husband. I actually did once, but only for a week. I don't think he even realized it. He thought I'd just gone on vacation, to visit friends in Florida." She laughed, not the elegant stage laugh my mother had perfected but an abrupt, spontaneous chuckle that made you at least smile if not join in. "Actually, I did go to Florida and stayed with some people we knew. I thought that's what you did when you left your husband. I told them Horace and I were breaking up, although I hadn't said anything like that to him. I just packed a couple valises and booked a flight to Fort Lauderdale. It wasn't all that common in those days—flying, I mean. Most people took the train. It was more elegant and leisurely. I must have gotten the idea to fly from a movie. I used to love the movies. I still do, but I don't go anywhere near as often as I used to. I must have gone to the movies three or four times a week," she said, slathering a second roll. "Horace worked late almost every night, and of course I had no children to occupy me. The closest I came was a miscarriage. I was thirty-three or -four. The doctor told me I had a tilted womb or something. Advised against any further pregnancies after the miscarriage. We considered adopting. This was right after the War, you know. Europe was full of DPs—Displaced Persons. But we never got around to it."

"Are you sorry you didn't?"

She stopped chewing for a moment, seemed to wait for an answer to occur but when none did she shrugged. "They're a lot of trouble, children. Especially young ones. But of course," she said, laying one of her elegant wrinkled hands on my own, I'd already spotted the big blue-white rock on her middle finger, if it was real it was worth thousands, "you know that already, don't you, my dear."

I told her how I got pregnant in my senior year of high school and how my father forced Tim Davis to marry me, how I resented being saddled with a young child when I was only seventeen years old, the stay out West when Tim was in graduate school. I must have rambled on for several minutes before I noticed her smiling impatiently at me across the small tabletop.

"I'm sorry," I said. "I guess I got carried away."

"Not at all," she said, but I could see she didn't really want to hear my whole life story, at least not all at once. "It sounds as if you've had a pretty rough time of it."

"I've had a few knocks. Some people have had it worse."

"Even so. You seem remarkably free of bitterness. If I had to endure what you have, I don't know I could have managed it with your equanimity."

Nobody ever accused me of being especially stoical before, and my surprise must have showed, because she said, "Perhaps equanimity is not the word I'm looking for. But you do seem to have accepted your fate remarkably well."

"If what you mean is I'm a glutton for punishment. This is not an isolated incident—what my husband did today. He pretty much treats me like this all the time."

"Like...how?"

"As if I were his child, his unruly child. He also makes life difficult in other ways I won't go into."

"With other women?"

I didn't say anything, but my color must have changed because I know my cheeks became warm.

"That's not so good," she said. "You've tried putting your foot down?"

"I made the mistake, you see, back when we first got married, of thinking I robbed him of his youth by getting pregnant. I tried to look the other way when he started carrying on with other women. Then I guess it sort of became a habit for him. After a while we stopped talking about it."

"You just accept it?"

"I could never accept it. But I don't see there's anything I can do. Unless I leave him, which I don't think I would do, especially if it means leaving Kevin as well."

"You could take your son with you."

"You don't know my husband. He'd fight me tooth and nail in the courts. He has some friends in high places."

She sat and stared at me, and I felt so ashamed for some reason I couldn't raise by eyes from the tablecloth. She reached across the table, put her hand on mine and began stroking the tops of my fingers.

"You poor thing," she said in a very different tone from the one she had been using. "You poor, sweet thing."

She gave me her card—I didn't think anyone really gave out "cards" except in Henry James novels—and told me I could call her any time. She also suggested we get together the following weekend for coffee. I said that sounded like a good idea, but I didn't give her my telephone number or even my last name, and as a matter of fact I never called her and after that day I avoided the part of Riverside Park where we had met.

Thursday, May 4

It's weird, the things you think about when you spend a lot of time by yourself. I'll be in the shower or just lying in bed looking up at the bit of sky I can see above Ninth Avenue, and suddenly I'm recalling something that happened fifteen or twenty years earlier as vividly as if it were in a dream. When I was spending all that time with Harry, I didn't think about anything but the present. Now it's as if everything I didn't have time to think about then are crowding their way into my consciousness like a bunch of people who've been waiting all day on line at a soup kitchen for their one meal of the day.

Like this evening, just as the sun was going down somewhere behind 18th Street, when I was suddenly back in Oregon, having lunch with one of the junior faculty members, a woman eight years older than myself, a local girl with a very high opinion of herself and, of course, of Tim Davis. She was pretty beyond belief, blond blue-eyed pretty, tall, leggy. She should have been in LA or New York making a living off her looks instead of working for peanuts in a jerkwater university town. This was before women's lib, when you could still entertain a thought like that without feeling you'd betrayed your sisterhood.

We'd been talking about, what else, Tim Davis, while chomping on a local mutation of a corned beef sandwich—a half for each of us. I don't even remember how we came to be having lunch, it seems so improbable. Where had I left Kevin? But never mind, there we were, in some soda shoppe on the town's main drag, something out of a Judy Garland-Mickey Rooney movie. She was looking confident in that effortless away only a woman with perfect skin and nearly perfect everything else can look, and I was feeling dark and dowdy, probably wearing some sort of house dress—I thought my ass looked too big in jeans.

I'd been telling her how I had to drop out of high school, my usual conversational gambit even with perfect strangers, not because I was of a confessional stripe but because that was the only story about my life I thought anyone would want to hear and because it seemed to me the only event in an otherwise uneventful existence. She had been listening to my account—I had it down to a routine as pat as any Borscht Belt comedian—when suddenly she says, "But what about you, Deirdre? Don't you have any ambition apart from your husband?"

You could have flash-frozen my face at that moment, I don't think it could have looked more surprised. No one ever made any but the most cursory of inquiries about my life—whether I liked the

Northwest (I hated it but couldn't say so), how long were Tim Davis and I married (I usually added on a year, as much to make it seem that he wanted me for myself as to cover up our shotgun marriage). If I hadn't had some ambition in mind for myself, however ill-defined, other than housewifery and childcare, I wouldn't have slogged my way through night school to get my Regents diploma and then dragged Kevin all over the CCNY campus for my BA. At the time this conversation was taking place I was enrolled in the graduate English department at the University of Oregon and would, before we came back East, earn most of the required credits for a master's degree. But this was the first time anyone had acknowledged, assumed I had a right to, a life of my own that was in any way equivalent to the sort of career everyone assumed Tim Davis would have.

I didn't dare say law school, although I hadn't yet given up my childhood ambition of becoming a lawyer. You have to remember, this was back when girls were still required to take Home Economics. So I told her I thought I might go into advertising after my husband finished up his graduate work.

Then she said something that was actually the reason why I was remembering this episode so many years later. "You know," she said, "you don't really talk like you're from New York."

She meant that as a compliment, which of course it isn't, besides which I know I've got a Bronx accent you could cut with a pizza knife. To this day, I don't know why she said that. If I could remember how we ended up in that drugstore in the first place, I might have a clue. But I can't remember ever talking to that woman before or after that day. I don't even remember her name. For all I know, my husband was sleeping with her—he'd be a damned fool if he wasn't and had the opportunity, she was that beautiful, I kept thinking all during our conversation. I'd almost be willing to believe I've made her up, that's how incongruous and isolated our meeting seems twenty years later. But I recall the heavy glass salt and pepper shakers on the black marble table where we sat, and the dry corned beef, as vividly as I can see the back of my hand as I write this. Only her beauty seems in retrospect to be possibly exaggerated, but that's because I always see other women as more attractive than others see them and see myself as uglier than I probably am. But otherwise, I'd stake my life that everything happened just as I've recorded it.

Did she mean I was too intelligent and articulate for her to acknowledge my Bronx roots? That everyone else who found my heavy
accent comical, though they pretended to find it charming, were mis-
taken? I didn't have a clue.

I said something about having to get home to my son and then
beat it out of there. I remember the woman—Angela, that was her
name, how appropriate—calling after me, "Can I give your ride?"

I never mentioned that meeting to my husband. It was shortly
after that, though, I told him if we didn't return to New York at
the end of the school term I would leave him. He had been offered
an adjunct position in the English department, it would only have
been a matter of time before he was made a professor with ten-
ure. Oregon would also have been a healthier environment in which
to raise Kevin. I didn't care. I wanted to be back on the streets of
Manhattan, to be near my mother. I doubt I actually would have left
Tim Davis, but I must have believed at the time I would because he
promised we would come back East as soon as he got his masters,
and that was what we did.

XVIII

A Walk in the Park

Friday, May 7

I finally got my ass out of bed and back to work. And none too soon, the director is retiring and of course none of my co-workers bothered to call to let me know. They had a dinner for him tonight, and it's a good thing I was able to show my face. They like to pretend we're all some kind of happy family, with Sid, the director who's retiring, as its father figure. He founded the agency back in the 1970s when heroine was still the drug of choice and there was plenty of government money to fund methadone programs like this one. I'll bet he's made a nice little bundle out of this place, but the official story is he's some kind of Mother Teresa who's dedicated himself to the salvation of junkies. I guess that's kind of a cynical thing to say. Maybe he did help some people. I don't really know, and to tell you the truth, I don't care. I'm just tired of working here, here and all the other not-for-profits I've worked for over the past two decades. They're mostly scams, just another way for someone to make a buck off the public tit, like most of the organizations that send me junk mail every day, everything from my fellow Jews trying to scare me into sending them a check so I don't end up getting stuffed into an oven, to politicians pretending they're not as crooked as the guy whose office they want to occupy. I say, a pox on all their houses. Anyhow, I ended up drinking too much at the retirement dinner and made a few jokes about Sid, the director, I probably shouldn't have. Such as who's he going to diddle now that he won't have his Puerto Rican secretary to bounce on his knee. Sonia is just a kid, barely twenty-one, and goes around in skirts short enough that you can see what she's had for breakfast. Mrs. Sid was at the dinner, of course, and I estimated, much to the amusement of my tablemates, it would take five Sonias to fit into one pair of Mrs. Sid's underpants. Not exactly what you want to bounce on your knee or adjacent nether parts while she takes a letter. Last place I worked, a not-for-profit in Queens that got city money to rehabilitate ex-offenders, the director had a creative, if not original, way of evaluating his female subordinates. They either went down on him or didn't get promoted, no matter how many years they were foolish enough to remain with the agency. Everybody knew what was going on, but to tell you the truth, the guy was a good administrator in every other respect and, as far as I could tell, a good family man too. I worked there six years and never got beyond account executive, the same level at which I was hired.

I must have gone over the line last night with my comments because at some point—I was too soused to remember exactly when—Barry, one of the older junkies who work as counselors at the agency, asked me to step outside with him. I like Barry. He's not just a junkie—ex-junkie, "recovering" junkie—he's also gay. I didn't go willingly, but I went, not realizing what he had in mind until he pushed me into the back seat of a cab and climbed in beside me. But I wasn't going to be pushed around by Barry or anyone else, so I refused to tell the driver where I lived, and since Barry only knew it was someplace in Chelsea, he ended up taking me to his place in the East Village.

"This is kidnapping in some states," I told him as I considered whether I could jump out of the cab in the state I was in the next time it stopped for a red light.

"So, tomorrow you'll have me arrested. And then you'll thank me for taking you out of that dinner before you got yourself fired."

"Fuck the bastards," I said. "Fuck the job."

"You won't be saying that when your rent falls due and you don't have squat to pay it with. Or maybe," he said, "you're independently wealthy and just work at the agency as a way to fill up your free time."

"Yeah, right," I said. "In my fucking dreams."

"So, there you go. In a couple hours you'll be fit as a fiddle, and in the morning everyone will be too well-mannered to say anything about tonight. Besides, you were only saying what the rest of us all believe anyway."

"Really?"

"Up to a point. I don't think Sonia actually sucks off Sid, do you? I mean, I'd like to think he had it in him, but what with his heart condition and his glaucoma and his bad prostate..."

"You left out his artificial hip!" I said, and we both had a laugh. Only, as a result I had a new problem. "Barry," I said, "I think I'm going to puke."

He got the window open in time for me to spare most of the back seat, but when the driver, an Arab or Pakistani, realized what was happening he started carrying on like I had set fire to the car. By that time we had reached Barry's neighborhood, so we just got out and Barry gave him something extra for the mess I made. The man took the money, then cursed us out in at least two languages. He called me a disgusting tart and Barry a pimp, two epithets which caused us both to double up with laugher and made me throw up all over again.

I felt a lot better after that second barf. I probably could have made it home on my own at that point, but I was enjoying Barry's company—we had hardly exchanged small talk till then—so I figured what harm could there be in going up to his place for a cup of tea. At least I wouldn't have to worry about his trying to tear my clothes off, and I dreaded going home to that empty apartment where there was nothing but bad memories to keep me company.

"It's simple, but it's clean and it's all mine."

"Its gorgeous," I said.

It was actually a bit overdone, too much like something out of a magazine, but a palace compared with my own bare walls and few sticks of furniture. "How can you afford it?"

"I pick up a piece of furniture here and there. Decor is my only vice. Well, almost my only vice," he said. It took me several weeks before I had decided Barry was homosexual, his behavior was that close to being straight. But once he came through his own front door he seemed to cast off his hetero persona. Finally he stopped fussing with our coats and clearing magazines off his sleek white leather sofa —fashion and home decorating journals—so I could sit down.

"Actually, it could do with a paint job. There's some kind of dampness seeps through the walls and even grows mold on them. I had a sealant put on, but it keeps coming back."

I couldn't see any mold, but I did spot a Picasso print I was fond of and went over for a closer look. Lu-Ann use to have the same print back when we were living in Oregon. I've never bought a picture in my life, though my mother's walls were plastered with them-- her own and her friends'--some of whom were quite talented.

"My sister gave me that for my birthday. Do you really like it? I still haven't quite made up my mind. Picasso is so, I don't know, old-fashioned, don't you think?"

I continued my tour of his big living room, I'd never been in one that was quite so grand, never mind one like it in a building that used to be a tenement. Someone must have knocked down a few walls to make so much space. There was an expensive-looking Chinese vase, a couple small but original sculptures, both of them abstracts, what looked like a small medieval tapestry and a carpet that was the color of saltwater taffy—I didn't dare walk on it in my shoes.

"Here," he said, handing me a cup of something hot. "Put this on your stomach and you'll be right as rain."

"How did you get the water to boil so fast?"

"Microwave," he said, sipping his own. "Modern science. Why don't you take a load off?"

I sat down on one end of the leather sofa, which was a lot more comfortable than it looked. "Don't mind my gawking," I said. "I'm just not use to being in places like this."

"Don't have any gay friends?"

I must have blushed with shame then, because he laughed and put his hand on mine. "Don't mind me. Us faggots are all self-conscious as hell. It comes with our victim status. Speaking of which," he said, "what did you make of that old queen who introduced Sid tonight?"

By now he had changed out of his suit and into something that looked like a dhoti. There was no question any more of his sexual orientation, but what had a little while earlier seemed amusing was starting to make me feel uncomfortable. But just as I was thinking I would go back to my own depressing apartment, my stomach turned and I barely made it to his kitchen sink before I brought up the herbal tea.

"I'm sorry," I said after I caught my breath.

"No problem. Here," he said, taking my arm and leading me back to the living room, "let me get you a pillow and you can stretch out on the sofa."

"I'll be all right," I said, but just as I said it a raging headache began on both sides of my head and I actually had to lean on him to make it to the couch without collapsing. "Jesus, if this is just a hangover, it's the worst I've ever had."

"There's a bug going around. Sheila had it last week. Put her out of commission for three days. Couldn't even get out of bed to go to the john."

"Just what I need," I said allowing him to take off my shoes and arrange a couple pillows under my head. I felt too miserable to worry about how I hardly knew this man. I felt like I might need him to call an ambulance.

He covered me with a homemade afghan and left me to look for some Tylenols. I don't know if he ever found them, because the next thing I knew it was morning—actually afternoon. I still had a headache, but it was of a more familiar kind. What wasn't so familiar were my surroundings which in full daylight looked more like a movie set than a place where someone actually lived.

I got up, splashed water on my face and checked the bedroom to see if I was actually alone. It was creepy being in the home of someone I hardly knew, especially after he had looked after me the way he did. It wasn't until I was pulling on my shoes that I spotted the note and key on the glass coffee table alongside the sofa where

I had spent the night, and apparently most of the morning. "Just shove the key under the door as you leave—or return it to me when you come to work on Monday, it doesn't matter. Hope you feel better this morning. Enjoyed our conversation last night. Will make your excuses at work—'stomach flu' sounds about right, *n'est ce pas?*"

Apart from a cotton mouth and a mild headache, I didn't really feel all that bad and could have gone in to work. But I figured why bother, Barry was already making my excuses, I might as well play hooky. I figured I could pay a visit to Emma—she was right there in the same neighborhood—and spend the rest of the day shopping, maybe take in a movie, anything but go back to my apartment.

What I really would have liked to do was meet an old friend and have a good talk over a pot of tea in some place like Schraffts, those havens of female respectability that used to be located so conveniently in neighborhoods where respectable women hung out, mostly near the big department stores. I used to turn up my nose at them and thought I would never be caught dead in such places, back when I considered myself as far from bourgeois as any young woman could be. No tea and scones for me until I was at least eighty. Now, though, I'd be happy to go anyplace where there was a sympathetic soul, someone like Emma, if she were only not tethered to a bed in that cheesy nursing home.

Then I got the notion that maybe I could do just that—not take her to Schraffts, I don't think there's any left in New York, but to a luncheonette, the Odessa over on Avenue A, maybe, for potato blintzes. Her husband used to wheel her around their old neighborhood. I could manage a wheelchair as long as I didn't have to haul it upstairs or lift her in or out of it.

It seemed such a reasonable idea, I wasn't prepared for the chilly reception it received when I proposed it to her keepers

"We're not insured for her outside the building," the troll in charge told me.

"I'll take full responsibility."

"If anything happens, a fall, anything, we may not be able to take her back. She could end up in a municipal hospital or in your own care on a permanent basis."

"Like I said, I'll take responsibility."

"What will you do if she has to use a toilet?"

"She'll go before we leave. I only intend to have her out for an hour at most."

"It's highly irregular."

She was a troll, but not a monster, and she finally relented. Emma was perfectly capable of sitting up in a wheelchair, I had found her that way on more than one visit. If she could sit in a wheelchair and watch television, she could sit in a wheelchair and be pushed down a sidewalk.

"Most restaurants are still not wheelchair-accessible," the troll went on, still hoping I would just go away. She no doubt preferred that her patients remained in bed full-time, comatose if possible.

"Look," I said, "I'll just wheel her down to Tompkins Square Park, it's just a couple blocks from here. It's a warm spring day. We'll watch the grass grow for an hour and then I'll wheel her back."

"This is all highly irregular," she said again. "You're not even a close relative."

"Close enough. I'm all she has."

She said nothing. Was it possible she actually had a heart?

I felt like I had been liberated myself when we were finally through the door and out into the bright sunshine of First Avenue. I raced her up the sidewalk, scattering pedestrians in our path.

"I feel like I did when school was let out for the summer," Emma said. "I wish I never had to go back to that place."

"I do too."

I slowed down once we were safely away from the nursing home. Emma didn't say so, but that fast dash to freedom must have been a little scary for someone who hadn't seen the light of day in so long. But she soon took a keen interest in the Jewish delis and other ethnic restaurants along the avenue, and we decided which ones we would like to eat in.

"I never ate Polish food, Deirdre. What's it like?"

"All I know is kielbasa, but I don't think I even had that more than once. Too much garlic."

"You don't like garlic?"

"Can't even stand the smell of it."

"My Ed was the same way. Wouldn't let me cook with it. And I love garlic so."

"Maybe we'll get takeout sometime and you can eat downwind from me," I said as we approached Avenue A. It was late morning, the swings and monkey bars—or whatever you call those new contraptions the kiddy parks are full of now, brightly-colored free-standing sculptures they look like—were full of kids with their mothers or nannies. I wheeled us over to an empty bench and put the lock on the wheelchair the way the nursing home attendant had shown me.

"Is this okay? We could move away from the playground if you like."

"Not at all. I like watching children."

I didn't. I can't stand the sound of children, especially babies crying. But it was such a beautiful day and I felt so good about having sprung Emma, I hardly noticed the occasional shrieks from the sliding pond.

"Ed used to wheel me over to Madison Square Park on Sunday afternoons when there was nobody there but locals with their dogs. I love to watch dogs. Children and dogs."

"Did you ever have a dog yourself?"

"Never. And of course no children," she said with only a slight alteration to her expression. "Just one miscarriage. Before my accident, of course. I would have loved to have a child. Spoiled it rotten. Take it to the circus like my mom and dad used to take me. Kids are great."

A bum—excuse me, homeless person—sat down on the end of the bench we were occupying. He looked harmless enough, but I remembered when this park was full of homeless people and they weren't all that friendly when they had the place to themselves, before the cops demolished their cardboard houses. This one wasn't all that old, younger than me, I figured. He had shoulder-length hair and a full beard, most of it matted with dirt. Probably some kid from the suburbs who decided to go native. He just sat and watched the children play. His hands were in plain view.

"What a glorious day, Deirdre. I'm so grateful to you for taking me on this excursion."

I wanted to tell her about my own adventures the night before, but I didn't feel like talking in front of the bum. There were half a dozen empty benches nearby, any one of which he could have chosen.

"Do you mind if we move?" I said.

"Move? Well, if you really want to."

"I think the air might be a bit fresher on one of the other benches."

Emma looked up at me, then glanced at the homeless guy.

"Sure."

I pushed her to a bench nearer the park's interior, but we had no sooner got settled than that same guy sat down on the other end just as he did before.

"Look," I said. "You've got the whole park to yourself. You have to sit next to us? We'd like a little privacy."

He didn't say a word, just sat there staring toward Avenue A like he was stone deaf. He had really got me pissed off. Crazy is one thing, if that was what he was. Rude is another. I know something about crazy, my own son used to be a mental case, but he would never impose himself the way this man was doing.

"Look at that dog, Deirdre. What breed would you say that was?"

"I don't know," I said, hardly aware of what she was saying.

"It's one of those firehouse dogs. You know, like in that movie?"

"I'd have them arrested," I said.

"The dogs?"

"Half of them are making a good living panhandling. They live better than we do."

I was staring at the bum, daring him to look back at me. Then I spotted a policeman heading across the park. "Good," I said. "Here comes a cop."

The bum was up and out of there. After he left, Emma said, "Did he upset you so much, Deirdre? He wasn't bothering anyone."

"He was bothering *me*. He has the whole park to sit in, but he had to plant his smelly self right beside us."

"Maybe he just wanted company. Maybe he was lonely."

But I was so angry I was trembling. It made no sense, but what does? We sat for another twenty minutes, but I never got back the good mood I had when we first set out on our adventure. I wheeled Emma over to First Avenue, and we window-shopped the other side of the street until it was time to bring her back to the nursing home.

"Let's do it again," I said.

"I'd like that."

"Next time we'll head over to the West Village. Maybe get some lunch and eat it in Washington Square Park."

"I'm game."

I handed her back to the attendant and kissed her goodbye—the first time I had kissed her, I felt bad about my getting upset over the homeless man.

XIX

Daddy's Funeral & a Visit

Not at the time, I was too full of outrage, but afterward, this evening when I was back in my apartment, I started thinking about my reaction to that man in Tompkins Square Park—I won't call him homeless, I don't know that he was or wasn't. Not whether I over-reacted, because I actually responded to him with great self-restraint, what I really wanted to do was have that cop arrest him. It used to amuse Tim Davis, the way I reacted to situations like that, such as when someone let their spoiled brat scream and holler in a restaurant. The cooler and more detached he remained, the hotter I became. "Kill it, kill it!" I'd say, causing quite a few heads to turn while the mother, who was totally at a loss what to do about the wailing child, having already spoiled it rotten, turned red with embarrassment. I still feel the same way, it's not as if I've mellowed, but I wouldn't show my feelings that way if I was in the company of someone like Harry who would probably be shocked by that kind of reaction, even though he would be just as annoyed as I or any of the other people who had to tolerate the noise. I hate that kind of hypocrisy.

I felt the same way about that pseudo-homeless man. If he re-ally was homeless, that was his business, I'm not saying he shouldn't be allowed in the park. But he had no business parking himself on the same bench as Emma and myself. He could see Emma was in a wheelchair and couldn't just get up and walk away like an able-bodied person. He was taking advantage of her crippled state, and that infuriated me much more than if he were simply coming by to panhandle off a couple healthy women who might fork over some change just to get rid of him.

But that wasn't what I was really thinking about this evening, though it was how I got started thinking about it--my father's funeral eight years ago.

Daddy died in Florida, which meant I had to leave Kevin and Tim Davis to go down to see him. My husband was still working at that time, or pretending to, I can't even remember doing what, and Kevin was in the middle of his exams. Daddy had only found out something was wrong a few days before the operation, so there was no time for me to prepare, I just had to get on a plane and go. He didn't die then, he died a few months later, which meant another trip to Florida, again without my son or husband accompanying me. They went down to visit him, to say goodbye really, in between my own solo trips. I didn't realize he was dying, or at least I didn't realize he was going to die so soon. Or maybe I did but didn't want to deal with it. I had a lot of resentment toward my father for a lot of reasons—for the way he neglected me as a child, then forced me into marrying Tim Davis, and because of the way he made my mother move to Florida when I still had a young child and a footloose husband on my hands. I blamed my mother for all of the above as well, but she at least was a woman subject to the same unfair expectations as myself. There was no excuse but male privilege for my father's attitudes.

I didn't stay until the end. My mother told me I could go back to New York, she could handle his final days on her own. We didn't know how much longer he would live, days, weeks, and I had the excuse of a job to get back to, I had a real job then, or thought I did. I felt guilty about leaving her. I knew my place as an only child was with my dying parent. But I didn't want to stay. I didn't want to be part of his or anyone else's dying. Plus I felt all that resentment toward him, though I couldn't let myself actually feel it at the time, not with him on his last legs. I told myself he would probably not die for a few more weeks, maybe a few months even, though when I think back to the kind of shape he was in the idea seems preposterous. I wanted to believe I would still have a chance to come back and say goodbye when I was more in the mood to, so when my mother said it was okay, I could go back to New York, I was glad to leave, glad and guilty. Now if I have any resentment it's toward her for not making me stay and do the right thing, what else is a mother for.

I got the news of his death from a telephone message someone had left on my desk, I was out of the office most of that day. "Your father passed away at eleven a.m. this morning." When I read it, I tried to remember what I had been doing at eleven o'clock that morning, but couldn't.

But I wasn't thinking about his dying when I was recalling what happened today in Tompkins Square Park. I was thinking about the funeral way out in Queens someplace, a part of the city I not only had never been to but found it hard to believe existed, it was so bleak and windblown. We traveled there with the hearse in limousines full of all my father's and a good portion of my mother's relations. It was like a gruesome version of Gatsby's trips to East Egg, or was it West Egg, through the ash heaps and billboards, I was thinking as I sat next to my mother who was dressed very elegantly in black. She and I and Tim Davis and Kevin had a limousine all to ourselves, a senseless extravagance, but my mother was paying top dollar for the funeral and that was one of the amenities provided by the schyster funeral home she had hired at the instigation of my father's doctor brother, probably because he got a piece of the action, the bastard.

Funerals are a dumb idea, but at least Jews get on with it without the interminable wakes Tim Davis's Irish relatives used to hold. I hated those affairs, and not just because I had to sit in a room with a corpse. What I despised was the way everybody gossiped about each other, and even about the stiff himself, just as if the dead person weren't right there with them. At least when you sit shivah—not that I've done it more than once or twice and then only to say hello and goodbye—the corpse is already in the ground.

They were all there: Bella and the quack, my father's brother Harold, his other sister Midge (who weighed 200 pounds and died six months after Daddy) and her husband the architect, plus their kids who were grown men and women of course, and a few of the grandchildren, all of them as ugly as the generations that preceded them. From my mother's side there were her sisters Fanny who married the coupon mogul and Rose who married the immigrant kosher butcher and spent her life behind a cash register even though she had a law degree from NYU. Her brother Lester, the only boy in the family, whom they all adored, was already dead.

None of them ever gave my father the time of day when he was alive, but there they were all turned out in chesterfields and black silk dresses. The men were wearing black yarmulkes, the only time they wore them was at funerals and weddings when they were provided free of charge. My father had put his doctor brother through medical school, but the only thanks he got for it was invitations to the bastard's wedding and to his children's bar mitzvahs, and then only because he was expected to, and did, fork over checks in four figures. He was never invited to their home, and they never so much as sent me a birthday card. I have no idea what his brother's obstetrical services to me were worth, but whatever it was it amounted to nothing compared with the sacrifices my father had made for him, toiling in the garment industry from the time he was old enough to get his working papers, giving up any personal ambitions he might have had for a professional career himself so the family could boast they had a doctor just like every other Jewish family.

My mother's people never spurned my father but neither did they treat him as an equal. Fanny used to invite me regularly up to her house in Westchester, and to please my mother I even went once, during Christmas vacation. But there was a big snowstorm that week and I panicked, thinking I'd never see my mother again if I didn't get back to the Bronx before the snow marooned me. I forced my aunt to drive me to the train station in a blizzard, my mother must have been very embarrassed.

We never associated with Rose and her kosher butcher, but that was because my mother couldn't stand her husband.

I was standing at the grave listening to a mousy little rabbi mumble the Prayer for the Dead. That's the last thing I remember. The next is Tim Davis carrying me, literally dragging me away from the gravesite, forcing me into the backseat of that limousine and ordering the driver to leave the cemetery. I don't remember screaming obscenities at my father's sister and brothers or calling them parasites and leeches or telling them to go back to their swanky houses and apartments so that I and my family could bury my father in peace. I don't remember spitting at my doctor uncle or calling him a Nazi pervert. I don't remember telling Aunt Bella she should burn in hell no matter how many kosher kitchens she kept. I do remember, just barely, poor Kevin shaking like he had a fever and my trying to fight off my husband who was forcibly restraining me from trying to get out of the limousine as we were exiting the cemetery. And I remember throwing up in the backseat. And that's all I remember.

I still tremble whenever I think about that day, just like Kevin, only my trembling is anger and his, poor little guy, was something else. It's no wonder he ended up a mental case.

Saturday, May 8

Kevin called, it was as if he somehow knew I had been thinking about him, though I don't believe in telekinesis or any of that paranormal nonsense. He could hear the tremor in my voice, he's like a very finely tuned seismometer. I told him I had been remembering his grandpa, without mentioning all that business about what happened at the funeral. He was very close to my father, even after my parents moved to Florida and he only got to see them a couple times a year. It used to make me happy to see how well they got along. I don't know why, there was very little I approved about my father when he was alive.

"Dad is sick again," he said then. "I didn't want to upset you, but I thought you should know."

"Sick with what?" I said, a surge of nausea rising as it always does when I have to deal with a crisis.

"The same thing. The infection's come back."

"He's in the same hospital?"

"I don't know. I just got home and found a message on my answering machine."

"From him?"

"No, it was from one of his...friends. I'm flying to New York in the morning, Mother. I was wondering if I might stay with you. If it wouldn't be too much trouble."

'Too much trouble.' That was Kevin all over. Never presuming, always self-effacing. It pains me to hear that kind of diffidence in him, I used to think he was just very well-mannered, because he should not have felt obliged even to ask.

That was last night. He's due in on a 2:00 p.m. flight. That should get him to my apartment at about 3:00, 3:30. I decided to go into work, to keep my mind off him and his father. That's where I am now, holed up as usual in my cubbyhole of an office.

The other staff, apart from Connie, gave me a pretty cool reception, not anything obvious like failing to return my greeting, just keeping their distance as if waiting to see what kind of odor I'm in with the higher-ups thanks to my behavior at the retirement dinner. That's fine with me. I couldn't care less what any of them think of me and will be out the door and never look back as soon as I can get my rear end in gear and find something better to do with my life.

Barry is the only other exception to the chilly reception I've gotten. When he found out I was here he made a point of stopping by to see me. I would have just as soon he didn't, I still feel embarrassed about getting sick in his apartment. But he treated the event as if it were an adventure the two of us were on together, found it funny even.

"I'll never forget the way Mrs. Sid looked when she heard you say her husband would have to start sticking it in a Coke bottle now that he won't have Sonia to diddle anymore."

I didn't remember saying anything about Coke bottles. I barely remember seeing Mrs. Korman, a stout middle-aged woman, ugly as home-made sin, wearing a gray silk dress that made her look like a high-rise draped in Mylar.

"How's the head?" he asked.

"Better. Thanks."

"You had a pretty good snootful."

"Did I? I'm sorry about...getting sick. There was too much garlic in those meatballs."

He laughed. "That must have been it."

I appreciated his solicitousness, both the night of the testimonial dinner and today, but I didn't remember anything that had transpired between us that justified the kind of familiarity he seemed to think he was now entitled to.

"Well, I'll leave you to it, then," he said, perhaps noting my change of attitude. It always amazes me when people react like that to my mood, I assume that if they do notice they won't take it seriously.

"Thanks again, for everything," I called after him, feeling bad about driving him away. But I was in no mood to be patronized, especially by someone I barely knew. God knows I would have welcomed a diversion at this point, what with the ordeal I have facing me after Kevin lands. Another trip to Tim Davis's sick bed is not something I'm looking forward to. But I can't—I just will not—let the boy down, not after all the years I neglected him when he needed me most.

Kevin insisted we go straight to the hospital, a development I was not prepared for. I thought we might have a cup of tea somewhere, drop his bags back at my place and decide how to proceed from there. I had no intention at that point of accompanying him to the hospital, never mind to his father's bedside. But Kev was such a wreck I could see there was no question of my leaving him on his own. He never asked that I accompany him to the sick room, but once we arrived at the hospital reception I could see that he was worse off than he had been when I saw him ambling toward me across the concourse of the Port Authority, a single modest-size suitcase in his hand. He seemed surprised to find me standing beside him as the elevator began its climb toward the infectious diseases unit, but by that point he was too agitated to realize what I was about to undergo on his behalf.

Tim Davis actually looked to be in better condition, considerably better condition, than he did the last time I saw him when he was on oxygen and barely able to speak. I was half-hoping we would find him unconscious, or at least too doped up to recognize us. Instead we found a good facsimile of the man I had walked out on several months ago, only made somewhat ridiculous-looking by the skimpy hospital gown he was wearing, sitting up in bed watching television.

"Hello, Father," Kevin said, quickening his step at the last minute to embrace the man, who accepted his embrace perfunctorily and more or less as his due, the way he's always received his son's affection, not to say adoration.

I watched them exchange some words until Kevin seemed reassured that his father was not nearly so bad off as he had feared. Then Kev turned toward me with bright tears running down his cheeks but a big smile on his face. "He looks well, doesn't he, Mother?"

I tried to return his smile, but as he spoke his father turned his attention my way and that was enough to make me feel as if my muscles were all about to be rendered permanently rigid.

"Hello, Tim," I managed.

He regarded me from behind his thick eyeglasses as though I were a specialist his son had brought with him to render a second opinion.

"You're looking well...all things considered," I added so as to break the awful silence. But still he said nothing, merely staring at me with the residual half-smile Kevin's embrace had elicited. "Maybe," I said to Kevin, my spine at that point feeling as if it was going to buckle like a child's tower of blocks, "I'll wait outside."

But Kevin would have none of it now that he had the two of us in the same room just like the old days. It flashed through my mind that perhaps he had planned it this way, that he might even have had some sort of reconciliation in mind, even that Tim Davis might be in on the plan. I hate duplicity of any kind, even when it's meant "for my own good." But I had nothing more than my own suspicions to go on, so I had no choice, it seemed, but to stay, at least for a few minutes, and I looked around for a chair to sit down on before I underwent the humiliation of collapsing.

Through the haze of my funk I saw that Tim looked a good ten pounds thinner than he did the day I walked out of our apartment on 121st Street. His hair also seemed to have more gray in it than I remembered. But seeing someone after even a few months can make you look at them more critically than you do when you see them on a daily basis. He was still a good-looking man, but for the first time I realized that his looks, just like my own, were not exempt from the wear and tear of time and that some day he would be an old man, perhaps better looking than most, but no less susceptible to sagging jowls and thinning hair—his own was already well up on his forehead, something else I had not previously taken note of.

Kevin sat down beside the bed and began to question his father about his illness and what was being done to treat it. My husband responded with clever non-answers, making puns and sarcastic remarks at every opportunity. Kevin laughed as always at his father's performances, but stuck to his original inquiries with a doggedness I had never before seen in him. Eventually he got some real answers: The infection was chronic and not responding to antibiotics as well as the doctors had hoped it would. They would be trying a new regimen of drugs this time around. No, he didn't know which antibiotics they would be administering.

The last thing I wanted was to be drawn into a conversation with Tim Davis myself, but I found that sitting there like some sort of ghost in the room was at least as stressful as having his attention directed my way, so I ventured a question about whether he had a fever. In response he turned toward me in a way that suggested he had been waiting for this opportunity all during the time he and Kevin had been confabbing. His glasses needed a cleaning, he never cleaned them until they looked like something that had been left in the sink overnight, but the smudges on the lenses did nothing to diminish the force of his stare. I expected him to say something cutting, but he replied in an even, reasonable tone.

"It comes and goes. Nothing like the first time. I appreciate," he added as if unable to resist his usual sarcasm, "your interest."

But I wasn't ready to be shut up so quickly. We were not alone in our apartment on 121st Street. This was a public place, he was a sick man confined to a bed. Our son was no longer a terrified child but an adult who seemed surprisingly able to hold his own.

"Have you had a second opinion?" I said.

His eyes narrowed, something that happened when he wanted an extra second to formulate a clever or cutting response. I had seen it happen when he was standing in front of a class explaining the Great English Vowel Shift (which I had had to drill him on for several days prior to his post-graduate final in Middle English), and at innumerable parties when he was working some pretty young thing into a dimly lit corner of a fellow faculty member's living room.

"No, I have not had a second opinion. If they can't distinguish one microbe from another, they'll probably end up killing me no matter what."

This was such an irrational response that I felt brave enough to ask a second question.

"How long do they expect it will take for the treatment to work?"

The skin between his eyebrows came together again, this time causing his entire forehead to wrinkle.

"I haven't asked," he said as if he were addressing a student who had called out an impertinent question from the back of the lecture hall.

But I was not his student and I was beginning to sense, thanks to the circumstances, that some of the advantage we had both always assumed he would enjoy in any interchange between us had, however temporarily, shifted my way.

"It's common practice nowadays to ask for a second opinion. It's your right as a patient, and it could make all the difference to your treatment. Of course," I added as I saw his mouth twitch impatiently, "it's your call, Tim. I'm only trying to be helpful."

"Thank you," he said. "Thank you for your concern."

XX

I Find my Hind Legs

Monday, May 11

I was bemused by my new role. Life with Tim Davis had always meant fear and subservience for me. Back when we were still teenagers I stood in awe of his superior intellect and overpowering personality, not to mention the way he seemed to attract the opposite sex like flowers attract bees. Later I lived in fear of losing him to one or more of those bees and consequently accepted constant humiliation as my allotted portion, I scarcely even let myself feel real jealousy. When I eventually looked for love outside my marriage I did so with a heavy sense of guilt despite the years of neglect and betrayal I had endured. By the time I worked up the nerve to leave my husband, I only did so because another man was ready to welcome me into his arms. I had never stood on my own hind legs and demanded what any self-respecting woman, any self-respecting human being, would feel they had a right to. And yet, there I was, sitting in that antiseptic hospital room, looking in the eye the same man from whom I had spent half a lifetime cringing.

I don't mean we didn't have our battles royal during the years we lived together. I can be roused, it seems, by only two emotions, fear and anger. Fear makes me want to hide, to get away, but anger, whether it comes from a sense of injury done to myself or, more often, done to someone I feel obliged to defend, literally makes me forget myself. When I'm sufficiently angry I'm a different person, I can stand up to anybody, almost anybody, and do so virtually without any thought for the consequences. But I only allow myself to feel that kind of outrage on my own behalf after I've endured what other women would long have put an end to by the more traditional methods of recrimination and nagging. I swallow my outrage and stifle my rage until it explodes, and when I reach that point it's best to avoid me altogether because I can be downright homicidal. I've actually taken a knife to Tim Davis, bizarre as that may seem, given what I've said about living perpetually in his shadow. We've wrestled with all manner of sharp and blunt objects, more so when we were young, but as recently as a year ago I threw a lamp, narrowly missing his head. He only laughed, causing me to feel even more furious, especially when he overpowered me, as he always has, then threw me down on the bed in Kevin's old room and proceeded to pull off my clothes and, shamed as I am to tell it, I was glad he was doing so, I was as aroused he was.

But the other day was another matter entirely. I was still very nervous, sitting in the same room with him, however incapacitated he might be, but I felt neither fear nor outrage as he and Kevin continued their conversation with occasional asides my way. For the first time in a very long time I felt like I could maybe hold my own. Even the occasional glances he darted my way, half-accusing, full of self-pity, did not disturb my equilibrium. For whatever the reason, I could see he was just a man—not a devil, a monster, a genius or a movie star—just a man, perhaps more troubled than most, but definitely life-size and not worthy of either my fear or contempt—though I had no intention of getting any closer than I was at the time.

"Don't you think, Mother?" I heard Kevin say without a clue to what he was talking about. "Dad says we could go up to visit Sarah. She would like that, don't you think?"

"I'm sure she'd be very happy to see you, Kev."

"When Dad's feeling better."

It was only then that I realized he meant all three of us. The notion was preposterous, but Kevin looked so happy I didn't have the heart to say it was out of the question. I would bring him down more gently when we were alone, assuming the idea did not die a natural death on its own. This was the little boy talking, the one who hoped against all possibility that his parents would kiss and make up and be like other parents. The adult Kevin would know better when he returned from the high he was on, seeing his mother and father sitting in the same room and behaving with civility.

I said I would think about it, which was literally true, I'd have no choice, but I had no more intention of going to see Sarah with Tim Davis—or going anyplace else with him--than I did of marrying Ghengis Khan.

The same nurse who had cautioned us about overtaxing her patient, poked her head in the door and gave us the two-minute sign as if we were all on a TV talk show. I immediately got to my feet, saying, "I'll wait for you outside, Kev. I need to use the john before we leave." Then I turned to my husband, ex-husband, whatever, and said, "I hope you're feeling better, Tim. I really do." He didn't say a word, merely stared at me as if I should wilt under the force of his censure. His reaction seemed to surprise Kevin, but it made me feel as if the real Tim Davis were back.

"Why did you leave us like that?" Kevin demanded before we were even out of the building. "I thought Dad was behaving very well toward you."

"I had to pee, Kev. Besides, there was nothing more for me to say, and you could see the nurse was giving us the high sign."

But he was sulking, a reaction that ordinarily made me feel guilty as hell but today just made me irritated.

"I only went in there because you asked me to. When I visited him a few weeks ago, he called me...well, he called me a name I don't care to repeat. Believe me, it was just a matter of time before he did the same thing today. You should be glad I left when I did. I might have saved you from a scene that would have left you a lot more upset than you are now."

But as we exited onto Amsterdam Avenue and a brilliant spring day, he still looked the way he used to when his father had been badgering him unmercifully, until the boy sat in his room and refused to talk to anybody. It was a state that eventually ended with his being carried out of the apartment by two thugs from Bellevue.

"Kev, you're not a child anymore. You are not going to get your parents back together by wishful thinking. You're not the first person whose parents broke up. You could even make a case that you're luckier than most, because your own parents stayed together until you were a grown man, although to tell you the truth you probably would have been better off if I left him sooner."

"How can you say that?" he said. "How can you say it would have been better?"

"Hasn't it ever occurred to you, hasn't any of your therapists ever suggested, that watching what your father did to me for all those years might have had something to do with your own mental state?"

He scowled at the sidewalk but said nothing. It was the same scowl, though in Kevin's case tempered by self-doubt, that his father put on before beginning one of his tirades.

"Do you think that was a healthy environment for a kid to grow up in? Do you think that was a good role model I gave you, allowing myself to be crushed by Tim Davis's bullying personality?

"I don't mean," I added, "that I didn't love your father or that I don't feel anything for him now even. I even believe that in his own way he's loved me as well. But the sort of relationship we had isn't a healthy one for two people to be in. Domination isn't any better for the bully than it is for the victim. I only put up with it because I didn't think I deserved any better. I blamed myself for his being the way he was."

"How could you blame yourself?"

"By my getting pregnant, for starters. I know, it seems like it was just as much his fault as my own. But I've always felt it was mostly mine. Kev, this isn't easy for me to talk about with you. I hope you know, however you came into the world, that I love the dickens out of you." I took his hand and squeezed it. "I really do. You mean the world to me."

We each said nothing as we approached the big gray monstrosity known as the Cathedral of St. John the Divine, Tim Davis's parish church once he gave up on Catholicism as unworthy of all he had tried to do for it. Some stone masons were hard at work at the top of its spires, trying to complete what had been begun decades earlier and then abandoned, some had thought for good. Their craft had even been thought forgotten until someone found one old man in Brooklyn who was willing to teach it to some young apprentices, and now there was a small cadre going around the country restoring other churches. I had read all this in the *Times* several years back but hadn't given it a second thought until now.

"Are you hungry?" Kevin said.

"Starving."

"Do you think that Hungarian restaurant is still in business, the one we used to go to for goulash when I was in junior high?"

"Right around the corner. Doing more business than ever. Should we have lunch there?"

"I'd like that," he said.

Wednesday, May 13

I received a letter today from Tim Davis, dated the same day Kevin and I visited him:

"I am writing to congratulate you, Deirdre. You finally have succeeded in alienating Kevin from me. I hope you are happy."

Short and bitter, and no split compound verbs.

Kevin said not a word about this supposed estrangement. When I asked what he and his father had talked about after I left the hospital room, he told me they discussed his job in Indiana and the prospects of the Yankees to win another World Series. He said he had left his father in good spirits, that they had even embraced.

Go figure.

XXI

Death & Denial

Friday, May 15

Tim Davis is dead. Even writing the words fills me with disbelief. I saw him just a few days ago. He wrote me that note. I know these are things everyone feels when someone dies unexpectedly. But this isn't "someone," is it, it's the man I've been married to for twenty-five years. You may as well tell me France or Japan has just ceased to exist, except I've never been to either of those places, so they could fall off the face of the earth and it wouldn't make the slightest difference to me.

Kevin is beside himself. He's sleeping on the cot here in my apartment just a few feet away as I scribble these words. He cried all night which, I guess, is better than if he had gone catatonic on me. He only fell asleep at 3:00 a.m. It's just passed 6:00 now, and I don't feel in the least sleepy myself, though I haven't shed a tear and don't know if I will or not. I know Tim is dead, I mean I believe it must be so, but the fact hasn't touched me any more than if it were just a bad dream Kev had. I remind myself the call he received from the hospital last night—it seems like last week—was unequivocal, but somehow it just doesn't register.

The infection suddenly "surged," they told him.

"Totally unexpected. They said Dad was making good progress. They thought the new antibiotic was finally kicking in."

I told him these things happen, new drugs are pretty iffy, and then realized what I must be sounding like, as if his pet canary had just popped off, which would have been bad enough, believe me, for someone like Kevin. But actually it seemed quite impossible to me that his father was dead. Even eleven hours later it still seems impossible, though I think I'm putting on a better face now than I did last night. I managed to fake some tears, but that was only because of the awful state Kevin was in. I still feel nothing myself, because I simply cannot believe Tim Davis is gone. A reality that big can't just be snuffed out the way you blow out a candle.

Ten a.m. Kevin is still asleep and I finally managed to drift off myself for a few hours. When I awoke with the western sky light above New Jersey—above where New Jersey must be, I can't really see beyond the spires of the theological seminary across Ninth Avenue—my first thought was I'd better take my umbrella to work today because it looks like rain. My second thought was I don't have to go to work today because Kevin has come to visit. It was only then that I remembered why.

Now I lie here on the same air mattress Harry and I slept on and did so much else on, suddenly a widow. I know some women lose their husbands a lot sooner than I have, during war, for instance, or to cancer. But in my mind widows are little old ladies in black shawls, and I'm not that kind of widow. Widows are also grief-stricken, and I'm not that either, though my eyes did fill up as I wrote the word "widow" at the beginning of this paragraph. Filled up but then cleared again like a drain that was temporarily clogged.

It's not as if Tim Davis died when our marriage still was a marriage, if it ever was, however much I once loved him and he loved me—I believe he once did. I suppose lots of women have found themselves in the same situation, women who go on living with their men long after the relationship has become little more than a habit or an obligation "for the children's sake." They preside over their husbands' wakes or shivahs as if the deceased had been their very reason for being, and I suppose in lots of cases he was, though a hostage can feel the same way, bond with her captor more genuinely than many of those widows ever bonded with their men. In the final analysis it really is an institution, marriage. You serve your time. You think death will mean release, even heavenly reward, then you find the very person you spent all those years resenting and not daring to wish dead is the only one you feel truly like yourself with. You've somehow become the thing you despised.

My mother was like that. Not that she despised my father, I doubt she did. But there was no question in my mind, even when I was a kid, that she looked after him—made sure he was looked after, usually by Sarah—because that was her duty as a Jewish wife. I inherited that sense of obligation from her, that was why I came back to Tim Davis when he conveniently broke his leg just a few days after I left him for the first time.

That was my excuse for staying with him when he was fucking everything that moved. It was my excuse for not making a life for myself until now. Between my sense of duty, my natural cowardice and Kevin, I didn't stand a chance of getting away, though I believe if Tim had shown me even a small fraction of the attention I craved from him I would have gladly stayed and never had a thought of leaving him. Someone, a family friend both Tim and I were fond of, once told me I was content with just a cookie. I actually took that as a compliment, an indication of how little I could survive on. But the truth was worse I lived on crumbs, and sometimes not even those. I lived on the moral merit badges I awarded myself for sheer endurance.

Now Tim Davis is no more and I'm Deirdre Davis in name only. It's virtually the only name I've ever had, I scarcely remember having any other, and even when I did it seemed as if I was spending those years as Deirdre Finley waiting to be christened with an identity that would establish my true self to the world. I never wanted to be anything but Deirdre Davis right from the first day my eyes and Tim Davis's met across two rows of students in Mr. Shoengold's American History class. At that point I didn't even know what his name was, that boy with the strange wiry blond hair—Jewish Mick, I used to call him back when he still thought I was a wit.

I was a virgin, and not just technically. I don't mean I hadn't fooled around a bit, but my sex life didn't amount to anything you couldn't show on one of today's daytime soap operas, or almost. But within a couple days after we first spotted each other in Ben Shoengold's class Tim Davis and I were lovers, at first in a lighthearted way, for the fun of it, you could say, taking every opportunity to step into an unguarded storage closet to kiss and grope each other a bit, but with an increasing passion that took us both by surprise. By the end of the week we had gone all the way.

It was all a revelation for me, though Tim had done it with other girls, with one at least. Many of my female classmates used to brag about having lost their virginity. It was a kind of embarrassment if you hadn't, but I kept such a low profile, my nose always in a book, that nobody ever threw my inexperience up to me. When Tim and I started up we caused a lot of snickering, but for me it was anything but a question merely of joining the club of ex-virgins. I had known all about how it was done, not to mention the variations. But I knew it the way I might know a bit of archaeology without ever having gone on a dig. I anticipated what was expected, but what was expected was never something I could have anticipated, despite all those years of playing with myself. Tim filled up my being the way his erection filled my vagina, and the sheer thrill of it—not just sex but love and sex combined so powerfully—made me frantic for him. It's a wonder not that we eventually were caught but that we could go at it the way we did for so long and not be found out.

Kevin stirred a few minutes ago, mumbling something in his sleep the way he did when he was still just a little guy. Then he rolled over and went back to sleep. He's sleeping with a vengeance, unwilling to bring himself to consciousness because he knows what he'll find when he does wake up. I envy him. There's no question of my going back to sleep myself. My brain is racing like I'm on ups, though I've never actually taken amphetamines, pot is the only illegal drug I've ever used.

Arrangements will have to be made. A Christian service. Tim is—was raised—a Roman Catholic, though he only went to Episcopal churches for the last eight or nine years. Kevin will deal with that. He goes to Episcopalian services and Catholic alike, though I've heard him tell people he's Jewish when they ask. Tim's father and Jewish mother are buried in a Catholic cemetery in Queens. I suppose that's the most logical place to put him. His brother is buried there as well--Ted, whom I could never stand, especially after he came back from Vietnam.

I wish I could begin to think about some of this as if it were real, but I simply can not. I can more easily imagine that when Kevin wakes up and calls the hospital they'll tell him a terrible mistake has been made, that his father didn't actually die at all, it was someone else named Davis. I'm aware denial is a common reaction to death, but knowing this and being free of it is not the same thing. Sometimes reality is just too implausible to be real. Tim Davis has dominated my life since my early adolescence. His life has always been larger than my own, subsuming mine even as I struggled against it. It's as if the sun were to go out. How could the moon go on shining? But it does continue to shine, however partially, ergo the sun can not have gone out.

XXII

Ripeness Is All

Tuesday, May 19

We buried Tim Davis yesterday morning. The only people present were Kevin, myself and a woman about my age who introduced herself as a "friend" of Tim's. A young priest from St. John the Divine performed the service.

I thought I would freeze to death before it was over, but I still haven't shed a tear. The "friend" wept quietly, wiping her tears away with a tiny lace handkerchief. Kevin broke down at the end, but once the initial bout of tears was over he was fine. Before we left the cemetery the woman embraced him with a warmth that suggested they were more than strangers with a common grief.

Kevin will stay at the apartment on 121st Street until he's finished sorting out his father's books and papers. After that he'll return to Indiana. He offered to move back to New York permanently, but I told him that isn't necessary, much as I'd love to have him nearby. I'm afraid New York would be too much for him, put him back into the state he was in two years ago.

Tim's death doesn't seem any more real to me now than it did two days ago, but I seem to be seeing him and our life together in a different way. Memories, things that happened fifteen or twenty years ago which I had come to think of in a fixed, unvarying light, now suggest other possibilities.

The memories crowd in, day and night, when I'm asleep and awake. I can be doing the most ordinary things, walking to the subway or eating a sandwich on a park bench outside City Hall. Suddenly I'm back in Oregon twenty years ago, only it's not me who's there but someone else, an objective observer seeing the experience for the first time, without the baggage of anger and shame with which I usually remember those days.

What I see is not the godlike figure I've feared and treasured all these years. I see a young man very unsure of himself, pathetically going from one woman's bed to another's to reassure himself he matters. I see a mind full of potential that would never be realized, not because the world was too dense to recognize it but because the man himself was too flawed, too burdened with self-doubt and conceit. I see someone very much like myself, very much like all the other bright young men and women who surrounded us. I see that the difference between their own success and Tim's failure has to do with a kind of knowledge that is just as necessary, perhaps more so, than what we call intelligence, and it's the very kind of knowledge I've always held in such low esteem.

I see how much Tim and I reinforced the worst traits in each other, pretending everyone else was either stupid or ill-informed. I see how much his half-cast Jewishness meant to him, how much he tried to live it down, not just for social or religious reasons but because he wanted to be like everyone else, to be someone he was not.

Kevin and I went out to get some late breakfast in a nearby diner. He seemed refreshed after his long sleep, sleep has always been a tonic for him. We talked about his plans after he goes back to Indiana. He wants to go on for a graduate degree in computer science. The therapeutic program he's in will help with the tuition.

"And after that?"

"Maybe come back to New York. I miss the city, even though it can be overwhelming."

My heart skipped when I heard that and I leaned across the Formica tabletop to kiss him. He's never been keen on my public displays of affection, but he made allowances this time. Then I started to cry, out of happiness at first, but then because I had all that stored up crying inside that hadn't yet found a reason to come out. Poor Kev didn't know what to do with me. I just sat and cried for five or ten minutes, the other patrons pretended not to notice. I went through tissue after tissue and finally had to use napkins from the dispenser on the table.

"I'm just so happy," I said stupidly when it passed.

It was only then that I realized he had taken hold of my hand sometime during my crying. It felt steady, self-assured on my own. If nothing else, I knew that whatever became of me Kevin would be alright.

"I hope," I said through some residual sniffles, "you find someone who really loves you and looks out for you, because if anyone deserves that, you do, Kev. I don't know what I would have done without you. Not just the last few days. I mean during the last twenty-five years. I guess it's never been a secret that I used to resent the way you came into this world. I still would have planned it differently if I had the chance to do it over. But I want you to know I never, not for a moment, would want anyone but you for my child, and I'm awfully glad I do have you, because I love you so much, Kev, I just do."

I started to cry again then, but not so hard. The other customers barely noticed this time, they were getting used to me.

"There's a Thackery exhibit at the Morgan Library," he said. "Do you think you'd like to take a walk over there? We could have lunch in the new restaurant in Bryant Park."

"Absolutely," I said, reaching for a paper napkin to dry my tears. "Absolutely."

www.ingramcontent.com/pod-product-compliance
Lightning Source LLC
LaVergne TN
LVHW042136040326
832903LV00011B/273/J